DATA MODELING OF FINANCIAL DERIVATIVES

A CONCEPTUAL APPROACH

Robert Mamayev

Apress·

Data Modeling of Financial Derivatives: A Conceptual Approach

ISBN-13 (pbk): 978-1-4302-6589-4

ISBN-13 (electronic): 978-1-4302-6590-0

President and Publisher: Paul Manning
Acquisitions Editor: Jeff Olson
Developmental Editor: Robert Hutchinson
Editorial Board: Steve Anglin, Mark Beckner, Ewan Buckingham, Gary Cornell, Louise Corrigan,
    Jonathan Gennick, Jonathan Hassell, Robert Hutchinson, Michelle Lowman,
    James Markham, Matthew Moodie, Jeff Olson, Jeffrey Pepper, Douglas Pundick,
    Ben Renow-Clarke, Dominic Shakeshaft, Gwenan Spearing, Matt Wade, Tom Welsh
Coordinating Editor: Rita Fernando
Copy Editor: Laura Poole
Compositor: SPi Global
Indexer: SPi Global
Cover Designer: Anna Ishchenko

Distributed to the book trade worldwide by Springer Science+Business Media New York, 233 Spring Street, 6th Floor, New York, NY 10013. Phone 1-800-SPRINGER, fax (201) 348-4505, e-mail orders-ny@springer-sbm.com, or visit www.springeronline.com. Apress Media, LLC is a California LLC and the sole member (owner) is Springer Science + Business Media Finance Inc (SSBM Finance Inc). SSBM Finance Inc is a Delaware corporation.

For information on translations, please e-mail rights@apress.com, or visit www.apress.com.

Apress and friends of ED books may be purchased in bulk for academic, corporate, or promotional use. eBook versions and licenses are also available for most titles. For more information, reference our Special Bulk Sales–eBook Licensing web page at www.apress.com/bulk-sales.

Any source code or other supplementary materials referenced by the author in this text is available to readers at www.apress.com. For detailed information about how to locate your book's source code, go to www.apress.com/source-code/.

Apress Business: The Unbiased Source of Business Information

Apress business books provide essential information and practical advice, each written for practitioners by recognized experts. Busy managers and professionals in all areas of the business world—and at all levels of technical sophistication—look to our books for the actionable ideas and tools they need to solve problems, update and enhance their professional skills, make their work lives easier, and capitalize on opportunity.

Whatever the topic on the business spectrum—entrepreneurship, finance, sales, marketing, management, regulation, information technology, among others—Apress has been praised for providing the objective information and unbiased advice you need to excel in your daily work life. Our authors have no axes to grind; they understand they have one job only—to deliver up-to-date, accurate information simply, concisely, and with deep insight that addresses the real needs of our readers.

It is increasingly hard to find information—whether in the news media, on the Internet, and now all too often in books—that is even-handed and has your best interests at heart. We therefore hope that you enjoy this book, which has been carefully crafted to meet our standards of quality and unbiased coverage.

We are always interested in your feedback or ideas for new titles. Perhaps you'd even like to write a book yourself. Whatever the case, reach out to us at editorial@apress.com and an editor will respond swiftly. Incidentally, at the back of this book, you will find a list of useful related titles. Please visit us at www.apress.com to sign up for newsletters and discounts on future purchases.

The Apress Business Team

*To all the people who believed in me and
encouraged me to publish this work!*

Contents

About the Author

Robert Mamayev is president of BinaryCurve.com. He has 15 years of experience as a data modeling, data warehousing, and data architect lead in the pharmaceutical, financial and government sectors. He is a trainer and developer of instructional materials in the field of data modeling. He is a certified Oracle Professional and holds a BS in computer science from Queens College.

Acknowledgments

I am profoundly grateful for the love, support, and constant encouragement of my amazing family, without whom this work would not have been possible.

I would like to express my great appreciation to the many other people who provided me support, encouragement, and advice during the writing of this book. I am especially grateful to Rebecca Stout and Joseph Licata for helping me edit the manuscript and to David C. Hay for reviewing and improving significant portions of the manuscript.

Preface

Endeavor always to conquer yourself rather than fortune.

—René Descartes, *Le Discours de la Méthode*

Recently I witnessed an argument between two close friends, both of them data modeling practitioners. At issue was whether data modeling is an art form. One argued that successful data modelers are a select and unique breed of software professionals whose skills cannot be taught; you're either born with them or you're out of luck. The other argued that practically anyone can be taught data modeling and become a successful data modeling practitioner.

I didn't take part in this discussion, preferring to stay out of it. As a dedicated student of Dale Carnegie, I know that the best way to "win friends and influence people" is to avoid such arguments altogether. But now is the occasion for me to open up and express what I feel on the subject. I do not consider data modeling to be an innate art. To me, data modeling is a learned skill that gets better and better with experience. Data modeling, like any other profession, requires dedication, practice, and passion. Most knowledge is perishable and diminishes with the passage of time unless continually refreshed and exercised. To become good at something and stay good at it, you need to practice and practice hard. It is through practice and action that you really learn things and become confident in whatever it is you are doing.

Introduction

It is not enough to have a good mind; the main thing is to use it well.

—René Descartes, Le Discours de la Méthode

The Purpose of This Book

The purpose of this book is twofold. On one hand, it introduces readers to the fascinating world of financial derivatives from the data modeling perspective and explains various rules that govern the world of financial engineering. On the other hand, this book stresses the importance of data modeling patterns and points out how to recognize, apply, and reuse them. This book is not intended just for those with a background in finance but for anyone with an interest in data modeling and business analysis. Data modeling patterns and the various strategies discussed in this book are widely applicable elsewhere, and the lessons learned here can be applied to projects in many industries besides finance, such as pharmaceuticals.

The Audience for This Book

This book is designed for two types of readers:

- Professionals knowledgeable about derivatives who are interested in techniques for representing and dealing with the complexity of their logic

- People experienced in conceptual data modeling who would like to use the analytical skills they have acquired to learn about derivatives

Prior knowledge of derivative instruments is not a prerequisite to read this book. I thoroughly explain every financial topic before I model it. Although you should have had at least some prior exposure to conceptual data modeling as a practitioner, a deep knowledge of data modeling is not required either. Chapter 2 will teach you all the techniques of data modeling that will be applied throughout the book to generate the models. Even if you are experienced in modeling derivative instruments, this book will teach you unfamiliar modeling strategies that you can begin applying in your own work right away.

Whatever your occupation and industry, if you can recognize and manipulate data modeling patterns, your career will benefit. Data modeling patterns are the industry-approved solutions to common problems found across various industries. These solutions have been tested and refined to the point that they are robust, simple, and intuitive. This book identifies the most important data modeling patterns and shows you how to apply them in practice. A knowledge of data modeling patterns, coupled with a thorough understanding of the underlying business rules, will result in high-quality and effective solutions that can be delivered quickly and on budget.

Book Structure

This book uses the *computer-aided software engineering* (CASE) methodology and *entity–relationship diagram* (ERD) modeling notation developed by Harry Ellis and Richard Barker.[1] After joining Oracle Corporation, Barker further developed and extended the CASE methodology, which was marketed as the Oracle Custom Development Method (CDM). To this day, Oracle's CASE Tools enable users to model using Barker's notation.[2] I developed every data model in this book using Barker's modeling notation and the Oracle SQL Developer Data Modeler (Release 3.1.4)—henceforth shortened to *Oracle Data Modeler*.

I confined myself to Oracle Data Modeler in the making of this book not to showcase a particular CASE product but because I found it to be the best tool to create ERDs that are easily understood, unambiguous, intuitive, and user-friendly. Every model presented in this book is a conceptual-level model. This requirement called for a data modeling product with a prebuilt library of industry-recognized, conceptual-level data modeling structures that readers could easily identify and understand. The Oracle Data Modeler has a prebuilt, out-of-the-box library of various conceptual modeling structures that perfectly suits the criteria for this book. For instance, the way the product displays supertype and subtype entities is very intuitive and highly detailed. Exclusivity arc, another feature I require, is readily available and has a high level of usability.

---

[1]Richard Barker, *CASE Method: Entity Relationship Modelling.* Addison-Wesley Longman, 1990.
[2]Oracle's original tool, Oracle Designer, has been replaced by the Oracle SQL Developer Data Modeler. In recent years, Embarcadero ER/Studio and Sybase PowerDesigner have made Barker's notation available.

Similarly, I use Barker's notation because it is intuitive and easy to follow. In the course of my career, I have come to the conclusion that ERDs created using this particular system of notation are the easiest ones for nontechnical users to interpret. By *Barker's notation* I mean not only the notation itself but also Barker's method of spatially organizing data models (Barker's *positional convention*). When you put all of these ingredients together, the outcome is diagrams that are concise and easy to read, interpret, and understand—as they must be to serve a useful function in the financial sector. Consequently, Chapter 2 is devoted to Barker's ERD notation and methodology. If you are already familiar with Barker's methodology, feel free to skim through Chapter 2. Even so, I recommend that you at least briefly review this chapter, because it is an excellent place to refresh your knowledge.

Chapter 3 introduces users to the world of financial contracts. It is important that you understand this chapter well, because it introduces key ideas and essential modeling patterns used throughout the book.

Chapters 4 through 8 discuss various financial instruments and coach you on how to model them. Each chapter is filled with modeling diagrams that explain each instrument in a clear and intuitive way. Chapter 9 puts the finishing touches on some of the key ideas and themes that recur throughout this book. The chapters build successively on each other and should be read in sequence.

The Benefits of Data Modeling Patterns

The ability to recognize and apply modeling patterns comes with practice and experience. In the first book of data modeling patterns, David Hay described their importance as follows[3]:

> *If you're going after things that are of fundamental importance to the business, you'll come up with things that are common across all businesses—people, organization, products, contracts are pretty standard in the world of commerce. If you use these as the basis of your organizing, you'll come up with a model which is concrete enough that people will recognize and understand it.*

A successful data model is one that answers the specific business questions posed today, yet is generic enough to anticipate the various changes that may happen tomorrow. Data modeling patterns provide you with the ability to create robust designs that are easy to extend and modify. A knowledge of modeling patterns leads to a more generic and stable data modeling design,

---

[3]David C. Hay, *Data Model Patterns: Conventions of Thought.* Dorset House, 1995.

one that anticipates changes. Anticipating changes when data modeling usually leads to designs that last longer and require less invasive alterations. If you model data, you are probably well aware of the fact that it is much easier to add a row to a classification table than to realize at some point after production deployment that a new supertype is required and an extensive recoding process is necessary.

If you build your models with the end customer rather than the technology in mind, you will notice how dramatically different your resulting models become. The progenitor of this approach, William Edwards Deming, was not a data modeler, but his core principles may be applied to data modeling as well as many other disciplines.

Deming (1900–1993) was an American statistician and business consultant best known for his "Plan-Do-Check-Act" cycle, more commonly called the Deming cycle. At General Douglas MacArthur's behest, he taught top management in postwar Japan how to apply statistical methods to improve manufacturing design, product quality testing, and sales in global markets. Deming correctly predicted that Japan would rapidly become an exporting nation of the most reliable and dependable products and services on the world market.

One of Deming's key principles was to delight paying customers with quality products and make them come back for more. His principles are built on common sense and go against today's prevalent short-term, "results now" approach. Deming preached that producers should build their products correctly right from the start, planning and developing products in a thoughtful and sensible manner before taking action. Once quality is in place, people will come back to make future purchases because they know that you deliver quality products. Companies in Japan stuck with Deming's principles and were greatly rewarded.

How can you apply Deming's principles to data modeling? If you have designed your model properly—generalizing and specializing when you have to, relying on data modeling patterns and best design principles whenever possible—your design will withstand the test of time and will not require any drastic alterations, leaving your customers happy and satisfied and leaving you rewarded and proud.

Think about the following: on a typical corporate project, time allocated to data model development (including end user interviews and documentation) is usually substantially less than the time dedicated to coding and testing the resulting system. No matter how brilliant the system code is, if the database is poorly designed, the resulting application will run slowly. End users tend to stay away from slow systems, so such systems are either retired prematurely or become candidates for major overhauls. Don't make this mistake by not allocating the proper amount of time to developing and fine-tuning the resulting data model. In the long run, you will be greatly rewarded.

The Conceptual Models Used in This Book

The data models provided in this book are *conceptual-level data models*, with all of the supertype and subtype entities left intact. This approach ensures that physical-level designs are responsive to stakeholder-approved business requirements. The identification of business keys, alternate keys, primary keys, and subtype/supertype transformations are all very dependent on the end user business rules. Including notions such as business keys and alternate keys in this work would complicate the main concepts and might mislead readers. My intention is to proceed with data modeling exercises as far as possible while leaving you space to experiment on your own. Remember, it is only through experimentation and practice that we really learn.

Another reason to keep the data models in this book on a conceptual level is to decouple them from any dependency on a particular database management system (DBMS) implementation. The DBMS that your organization adopts for your particular project will have numerous unique features that may favor a particular implementation approach. As a consultant, I have worked with numerous DBMSs, and their unique functionalities have dictated some of the decisions I've made when translating my conceptual models into logical and eventually physical models. These decisions have nothing to do with the conceptual data model, which needs to stay neutral with respect to and independent of various implementation methods. Even though a majority of my career was spent working with the Oracle DBMS, my conceptual models have stayed database-neutral. This book is built on the same precept.

Practice and Dedication

How do you get to Carnegie Hall? Only through practice and dedication. The same should be said about becoming proficient in data modeling. To master new data modeling techniques, you need to practice and practice hard. In life you may come across data modeling practitioners who seem to know a great deal about data modeling but do little to show their skills. Inadvertently, they become passive observers or passengers, simply modeling the things they see without applying any creativity and imagination. Passive modeling does work, but it is very limiting because it leads to rigid models that are resistant to change. Creative data modeling, on the other hand, leads to models that are easy to modify because their designers have built them with change in mind. Practice creative modeling by asking questions and by not being afraid to ask questions. By asking questions you gain a deeper understanding of the subject area and an advantage over passive modelers that comes from your fresh eyes and unbiased opinions.

Practice is doubly important because it provides you with business stake-holder feedback and encourages you to try different things. Without practice, your skills diminish and perish. With practice you will be able to take your modeling skills to even more creative and innovative levels. Knowledge and practice are not enough by themselves to produce the best results. Practice without passion produces results that are lackluster and ordinary. To be the best at what you do, you need to have a passion for the job. Passion will drive you to be the best at what you do and always perform at your peak level.

Asking the Right Questions

Most projects involve some element of the unfamiliar. Typically, this small chunk of the project is associated with deadlines and other pressures. Some people rise to the challenge, but others underperform. In situations like these, you need to realize that you cannot deliver a quality solution without a proper understanding of the underlying business rules. There will always be someone on your project who has the answers to your questions. Quite often your task as a data modeler is to find these subject matter experts, interview them, and ferret out as much information as possible. Getting information from people is an art, and you should practice it as often as possible.

First, it is okay to admit to subject matter experts that your knowledge in a particular subject area is limited; this kind of admission typically disarms the other party, making them feel more sympathetic to your needs, more impor-tant, and thus more talkative.

When you interview subject matter experts, minimize *close-ended questions* that lead to quick yes or no answers, because they impede the flow of fer-tile conversational exchange. Instead, ask *open-ended questions* fashioned to encourage full disclosure and meaningful discussion. For instance, asking a subject matter expert to explain a particular business process will facilitate a high-quality and productive discussion.

Conclusion

This chapter discussed a variety of topics, ranging from the overall structure of this book to the importance of being able to recognize and apply various modeling patterns. It emphasized that an eagerness to learn and a desire to gain new information are both key qualities if one hopes to find success in this industry, and that passively receiving information is not enough. Only through repeated practical applications of knowledge can we learn things and become successful. By being fearless when it comes to asking questions, we are able to master any particular business area. Finally, do it with passion or not at all!

Recommended Reading

Date, C.J. Database in Depth: Relational Theory for Practitioners. O'Reilly Media, 2005.

Halpin, Terry, and Tony Morgan. Information Modeling and Relational Databases, 2nd ed. Morgan Kaufmann, 2008.

Barker's Notation

Divide each difficulty into as many parts as is feasible and necessary to resolve it.

— René Descartes, *Le Discours de la Méthode*

This chapter introduces Barker's computer-aided software engineering (CASE) methodology, stressing its main points, summarizing its key strategies, and emphasizing the importance of aesthetic conventions. It will not go into unnecessary depth, in as much as the methodology is the foundation but not the main focus of this book. This chapter equips you with the basic knowledge you will need to feel comfortable using the various conceptual diagrams presented throughout the book. The first section lays out some basic definitions and an explanation of some of the key features of Barker's notation.

Different Types of Data Models

Practitioners split data modeling into two branches: *conceptual data modeling* and *structural data modeling*. The entity–relation diagrams (ERDs) in this book all belong to the realm of conceptual data modeling. The entity–relationship modeling techniques for creating ERDs were pioneered by Peter Chen.[1]

---

[1]Peter Pin-shan Chen, "The Entity-Relationship Model: Toward a Unified View of Data," *ACM Transactions on Database Systems* (1976), 9–36.

Conceptual data modeling performs the following functions:

- Describes the enterprise without regard for the kinds of technology that might be used to implement a database

- Describes the entities of significance to the enterprise and the relationships among them, specifically named to represent pairs of clear assertions about the nature of the enterprise

Structural data modeling is used in software engineering to graphically represent database structures and the various relationships between them. This data modeling type is subdivided into two subtypes:

- The *logical data model* describes data in terms of the data management technology that will be used: relational tables and columns, object-oriented classes and attributes, XML tags, and so forth.

- The *physical data model* specifically describes how data will be stored on various storage media.[2]

Every data model consists of three aspects: *entities*, *attributes*, and the *relationships* among them. These aspects are considered in the following sections.

Entity

An *entity* is "a thing of significance about which an enterprise wishes to hold information."[3] It is something that is of the uttermost importance to a business, something the business values and cherishes. It may be the product the business produces or the service the business performs. Whereas an entity is a thing of interest, an *entity type* is a defined set of entities.

In Barker's notation, an entity should be shown with the following specifications (Figure 2-1):

1. A rectangle with rounded corners

2. Entity name in uppercase letters

3. Entity name not in singular (not plural) form

4. Entity name inside the entity rectangle

---

[2]David C. Hay, "Kinds of Data Models and How to Name Them," Essential Strategies, 2012. PowerPoint presentation available at http://www.youtube.com/watch?v=PU7nKBNR1Vs.
[3]Richard Barker, *CASE Method: Entity Relationship Modelling*. Addison-Wesley Longman, 1990.

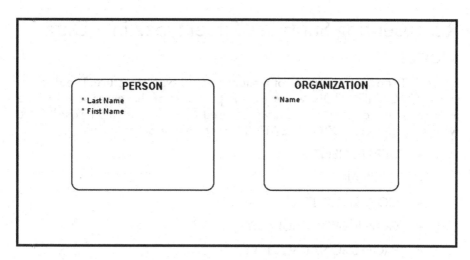

Figure 2-1. Two sample entities represented according to Barker's specifications

If an entity represents something of importance to an organization, then an *entity instance* is a row that is stored within the entity. In Figure 2-1, a PERSON is an entity and the specific record stored within it (with Last Name = "Smith" and First Name = "Billy") is the entity instance.

Subtypes and Supertypes

You will often encounter entity types whose instances are also instances of a more general type as well. In the data modeling world, the first group of instances is called a *subtype* of the second group. The second group is called a *supertype*.[4] This is represented in the Barker's notation by a subtype being shown *inside* its supertype. When you make a supertype, you artificially create a container for the like things.

---

[4] To be fully "buzzword-compliant" (David C. Hay's expression), you should know that this supertype/subtype structure is known as *specialization*.

Representing Subtypes/Supertypes in a Data Model

Figure 2-2 shows an example of a supertype/subtype structure. The diagram shows ORGANIZATION, which for the purposes of this exercise we define as "a collection of people who have gathered to accomplish a purpose." Here we assert that each ORGANIZATION must be one of the following:

- DEPARTMENT
- COMPANY
- GOVERNMENT
- GOVERNMENT AGENCY
- PROFESSIONAL SOCIETY
- OTHER ORGANIZATION

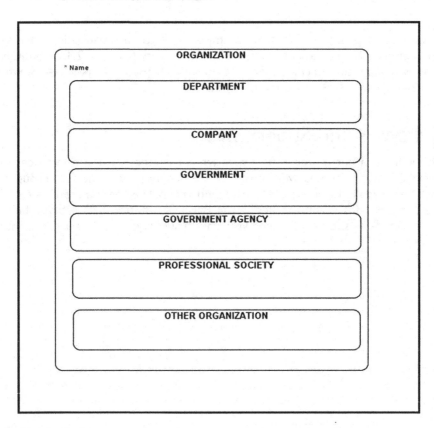

Figure 2-2. An Organization supertype

Note that this diagram also asserts that by definition, each instance of a DEPARTMENT must be also an instance of an ORGANIZATION, each instance of a COMPANY must be also an instance of an ORGANIZATION, and so forth.

In Figure 2-3, subtypes PERSON and ORGANIZATION are contained within the supertype PARTY. The ability to create hierarchies of various levels (or depths) in a conceptual data model is a powerful tool that adds flavor and meaning to the design. With the help of supertype/subtype entities, we are able to articulate certain relationships and display certain business rules that would otherwise be difficult to show in a conceptual model. The ability to establish hierarchical relationships between various entities not only simplifies the design but improves the articulation of the underlying business rules and makes the model less ambiguous and more meaningful.

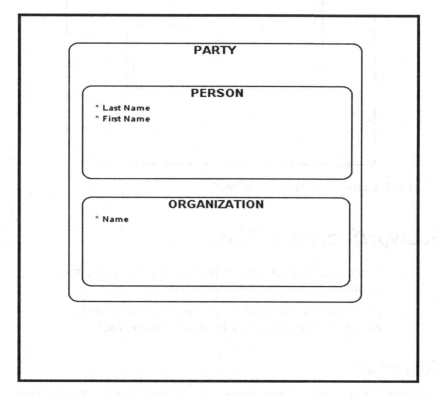

Figure 2-3. Example of a simple hierarchy

Note that attributes and relationships of the supertype apply to all of its subtypes. Every subtype *inherits* these common attributes and relationships. On the other hand, any attributes and relationships shown for a subtype are unique to that subtype. These unique attributes and relationships are not shared among the subtypes, nor do they apply to the supertype.

In general, a supertype/subtype structure should not contain only one subtype, implying identity. If there might be other subtypes, you can say that with a second indeterminate subtype. In Figure 2-4, for example, an ASSET TYPE is shown to be either a CURRENCY ASSET CLASS TYPE or an OTHER ASSET TYPE.

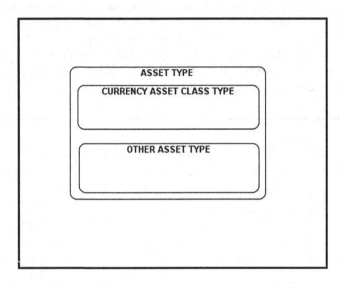

Figure 2-4. Subtypes/supertypes in a data model

Subtype/Supertype Rules

1. Every entity instance of a supertype must be an instance of one of its subtypes (*exhaustive rule*).

2. Every entity instance of a supertype must be an instance of only one entity subtype (*mutually exclusive rule*).

Attributes

An attribute is a property of an entity type that describes a particular characteristic of that entity type. The property takes a value for each instance of that entity type. Attributes cannot exist by themselves and should be discussed within the context of an associated entity. An attribute will be one of three types (see Figure 2-5):

1. Unique identifier (UID), which uniquely identifies an entity instance. UIDs are implemented as primary keys.

2. Mandatory attributes, which cannot be NULL.

3. Nonmandatory or optional attributes.[5]

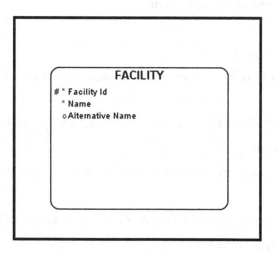

Figure 2-5. Entity attributes

According to the conventions supported by Barker's notation:

1. A *column name* is preceded by a special symbol:

   # denotes a key attribute

   * denotes a mandatory attribute

   o denotes an optional (nonmandatory) attribute

2. Column Name is written with the first letter of each word in uppercase.

Try to avoid any ambiguities when creating column names. Column names should be nonambiguous and readable; thus, avoid extreme abbreviations.

---

[5]In database technology parlance, these attributes are *nullable*.

Relationships

Each *relationship* represents two strong assertions about the two entity types involved. The relationship names are defined so that the relationships in each direction can be read as a common English statement. Specifically, the resulting sentences have the following structure:[6]

Each

<subject entity type name>

Must be   (If the half-line next to the subject entity type is *solid*)

(or)

May be   (If the half-line next to the subject entity type is *dashed*)

<relationship name>

One or more (…if there is a "crow's foot" (>) next to the object entity type)

(or)

One and only one (…if there is no "crow's foot" next to the object entity type.)

<object entity type name>

In Figure 2-6, we establish a relationship between PARTY and PARTY ADDRESS entities. In Barker's notation, a mandatory relationship is depicted by a solid line; a nonmandatory relationship is described by a dashed line. The relationship in Figure 2-6 states that:

> "Each PARTY may be *located in* one or more PARTY ADDRESSES."

> "Each PARTY ADDRESS must be *for* one and only one PARTY."

---

[6]David C. Hay, personal communication.

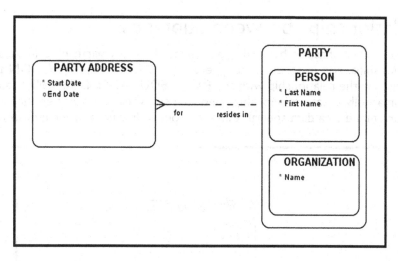

Figure 2-6. A sample relationship

David C. Hay underscores the importance of selecting appropriate relationship names:[7]

The important insight that Harry Ellis and Richard Barker brought to this field was not the notation (although it really is the best one), but the notion that the model is the graphic representation of a set of natural language assertions about the nature of the enterprise. The graphics are just a way to take notes. If you are clever in creating the relationship names—not a trivial point, by the way—you will have a set of assertions that the subject matter experts must agree with or disagree with.

Rules Governing Relationships

Following are the rules governing relationships when using Barker's notation:

- A relationship may exist between a maximum of two entities.
- An entity may have a relationship with itself (called a recursive relationship).
- A relationship has two perspectives.
- Each perspective of a given relationship should be labeled.

---

[7]David C. Hay, personal communication.

Relationships between Subtypes

Figure 2-7 emphasizes how subtypes themselves can participate in various relationships. For instance, a subtype of the PARTY called a PERSON participates in the relationship with the PARTY EDUCATION. The ability to diagrammatically create relationships between subtypes and other entities is an important aid to a data specialist and is a tool widely used in the industry.

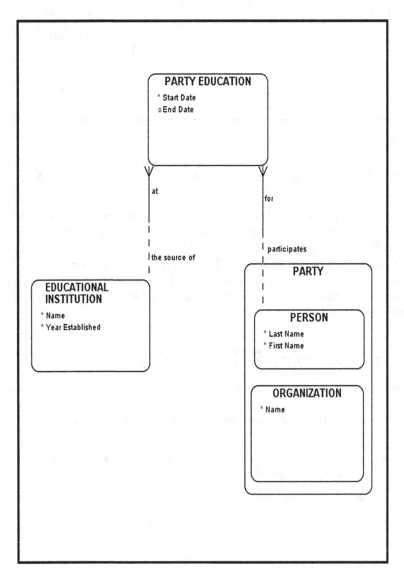

Figure 2-7. Recording subtype relationships

A more complicated and nuanced situation that often confuses novice modelers is depicted in Figure 2-8. Here we have established relationships between two subtypes of the same supertype. A PERSON and an ORGANIZATION form an employment relationship (represented in the model by an entity called EMPLOYMENT). But what if your business requirement allows for an ORGANIZATION to participate in an employment relationship with another ORGANIZATION? This situation may arise in the real world, where one company subcontracts with another company to do work. In this case, the relationship between the EMPLOYMENT and PERSON entities should be modified to a relationship between the EMPLOYMENT and PARTY entities to make the relationship more generic.

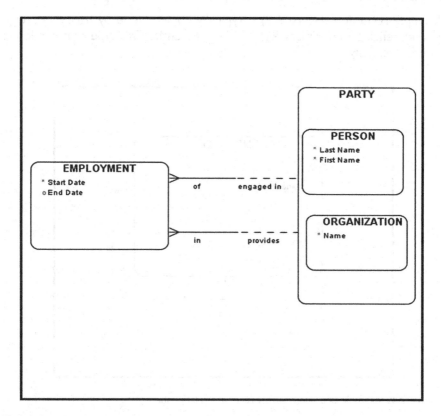

Figure 2-8. Relationship between subtypes

What about a business rule that states that under certain circumstances a PARTY may employ another PARTY? In such a case, we would probably want to establish two relationships between PARTY and EMPLOYMENT, thus allowing any subtype of a PARTY to participate in an employment relationship with another PARTY.

Modeling Recursive Relationships

Self-referencing relationships are very important in data modeling. They are grouped into three main classes:

- Recursive many-to-many relationships
- Recursive one-to-many relationships
- Recursive one-to-one relationships

Recursive One-to-Many Relationships

A simple recursion (Figure 2-9) is typically implemented by having a foreign key referencing the primary key of the same entity. This type of recursion is called a *hierarchy*.

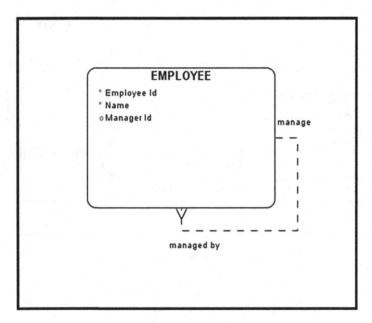

Figure 2-9. Example of a one-to-many recursive relationship

The recursive relationship in Figure 2-9 may be read as:

- Each employee may manage one or more employees
- Each employee may be managed by one and only one employee

Implementing one-to-many recursive relationships in DBMS is relatively straightforward. Table 2-1 diagrams a solution by having a foreign key referencing the primary key of the same entity.

Table 2-1. Implementing a One-to-Many Recursive Relationship

Employee id	Name	Manager id
1	Joe	
2	Tony	1
3	Robert	1
4	Richard	2
5	Jane	2
6	Lisa	3
7	Alex	3
8	Ben	5
9	Mark	5
10	Lan	6

Recursive Many-to-Many Relationships

Another type of recursive relationship that is very important in data modeling is the recursive *many-to-many* (M:N) relationship. The structure of this relationship is illustrated in Figure 2-10.

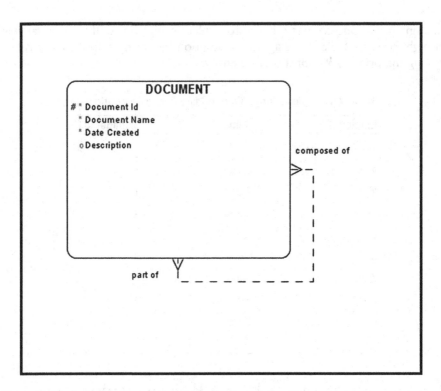

Figure 2-10. Example of a many-to-many recursive relationship

The diagram may initially appear confusing, but it is easy to interpret when you remember that each DOCUMENT may consist of other DOCUMENTS (or subdocuments). Then each DOCUMENT (incorporating any number of subdocuments) may itself be part of a set of documents making up another, larger DOCUMENT.

Recursive many-to-many relationships typically cannot be handled directly by modern DBMS and must be translated instead into two familiar one-to-many relationships using a STRUCTURE entity. The diagram in Figure 2-11 depicts a general solution to the recursive M:N relationship using the STRUCTURE entity. Note that the model in Figure 2-11 is often called a *bill of materials* (BOM) structure.

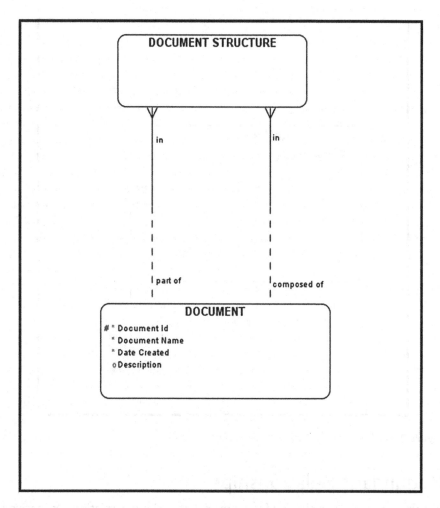

Figure 2-11. Resolving the many-to-many recursive relationship using a structure entity

Here, a recursive many-to-many relationship is transformed into two one-to-many relationships with the help of a DOCUMENT STRUCTURE entity. Note that the two relationships coming from the DOCUMENT STRUCTURE entity are mandatory.

Recursive One-to-One Relationships

A recursive *one-to-one* relationship is called a *chain* (Figure 2-12), in which one entity instance may be associated with at most one other entity instance in either direction.

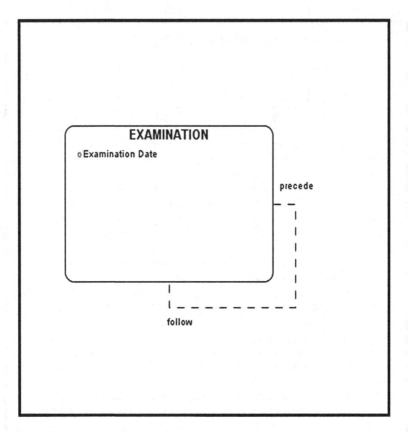

Figure 2-12. Recursive one-to-one relationship

Redundant Relationships

In some cases, a spot check of your model may show a relationship derived from another already-existing relationship in the model. This relationship is called a *redundant relationship*; it should be removed from your model, along with any associated documentation that you may have created.

Figure 2-13 shows a redundant "located in" relationship between the ORGANIZATION and the COUNTRY entity; this relationship is redundant because the same information can be deduced from the relationships between the ORGANIZATION and CITY and the CITY and COUNTRY entities.

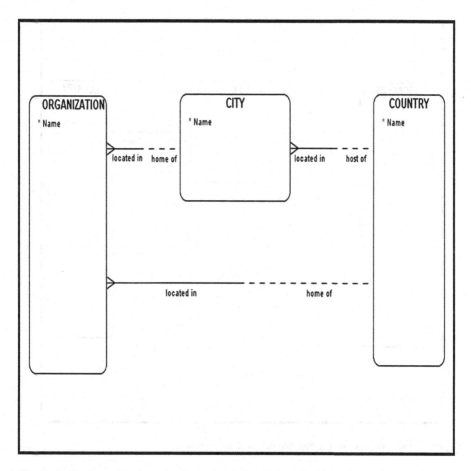

Figure 2-13. Example of a redundant relationship (before the change)

Figure 2-14 shows the same information as before, with the redundant relationship removed. Make sure to properly document your reasoning and findings before physically removing any relationship.

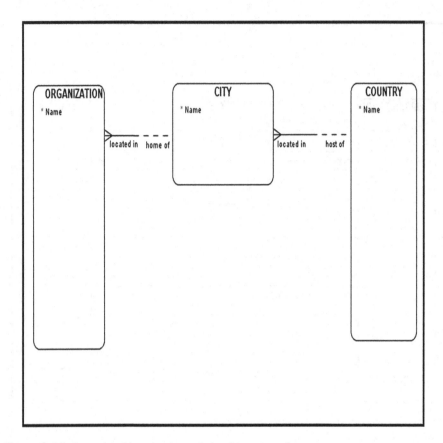

Figure 2-14. Example with redundant relationship removed

Situations may arise where a relationship you need to remove is semantically different and thus cannot be logically deduced from an already-existing relationship. In general, semantics is a subfield of linguistics that studies the meanings of words. In addition, *semantics* has been widely adopted as a term used in theoretical computer science to refer to the meaning of languages, as opposed to that language's form (*syntax*). This book, uses *semantics* in the linguistic sense of a word in reference to precisely defining the meanings of the words used in models.

For instance, assume that the "located in" relationship between ORGANIZATION and COUNTRY is replaced with the "country of origin" relationship. It is possible that a given company was founded in country A and later was purchased by another party based in country B. The company in question may want to preserve the country of origin information to reconstruct its past history. In this case, the "country of origin" relationship represents a valuable piece of business information and should be preserved.

In general, before removing anything from your data model (including any relationships), consult with the project stakeholders and subject matter experts regarding the validity of the relationship in question. Make sure your model and the underlying documentation have properly captured the meaning of each and every relationship (including the one in question). Only once a redundant relationship has been confirmed by all involved parties (aka *stakeholders*—the various subject matter experts, business analysts, and so forth) may you safely remove it from your data model and the underlying documentation.

In every diagram up to this point, the entities on the "many" end of each relationship (your typical "transactional" entities) have been positioned either to the left or above the reference entities. I have constructed the models in this way because this *positional convention* forms the crux of Barker's positional convention methodology. I discuss this convention further a little later in this chapter.

Exclusivity Arc

Consider the following business requirement as one you might have to model:

> A pier must be owned either by a seaport authority (SA) or by a charter boat association (CBA). Both a seaport authority and a charter boat association may own more than one pier. Once owned by a party, a pier cannot be resold.

Your first attempt to model this requirement will be through the use of subtype/ supertype entities (Figure 2-15). However, the subtype/supertype approach would not be useful here because neither a SEAPORT AUTHORITY nor a CHARTER BOAT ASSOCIATION can be generalized into a PIER. Similarly, a SEAPORT AUTHORITY is not a specialization of a PIER. You may safely conclude, then, that the model presented in Figure 2-15 would be unusable because it doesn't show a valid hierarchy, which is necessary to create a subtype/supertype relationship.

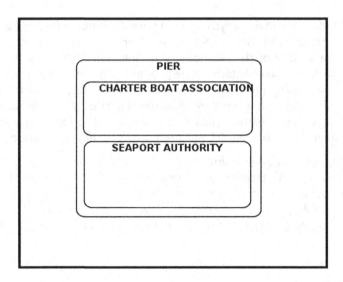

Figure 2-15. Illogical subtype (incorrect approach)

An alternative approach is modeled in Figure 2-16. According to the diagram, a PIER must be owned either by a SEAPORT AUTHORITY or a CHARTER BOAT ASSOCIATION, but not both. An *exclusivity arc* allows you to show in the model without any ambiguity a business rule clearly indicating that only one of these multiple relationships will be valid at any one time.

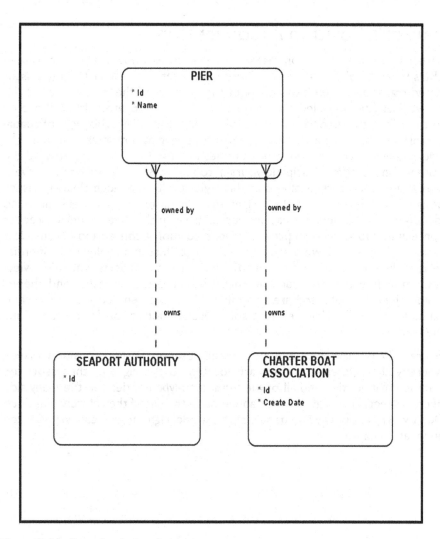

Figure 2-16. Example of an exclusivity arc

An entity to which an exclusivity arc relationship applies is called a *target entity*. In the example, PIER is the target entity. An exclusivity arc should intersect at a minimum of two relationships. Your target entity will store the foreign keys that point back to the entities affected by the exclusivity arc. In our case, PIER will end up storing the foreign keys for the SEAPORT AUTHORITY and CHARTER BOAT ASSOCIATION entities.

Barker's Positional Convention

Barker's *positional convention* methodology addresses how it is easier to read ERDs when all of the reference entities are located to the right of the associated transactional entities and all of the entities on the "many side" of the crow's feet (the so-called transactional entities) are located either above or to the left of the associated reference entities. Essentially, this type of spatial organization allows the viewer to begin processing data models from the right side, beginning with the reference entities and eventually moving toward the transactional entities. Discipline yourself to follow Barker's positional convention, and you will soon realize that this style results in a much cleaner, crisper design. These highly readable designs make it easier for your end users to identify various problem areas and logical flaws in the data model. Moreover, nontechnical folks tend to prefer Barker's positional convention because it is easier to follow; reviewers are less likely to get lost in a spider web of entity relationships. Keep in mind that many subject matter experts who will review your models will not be familiar with ERD modeling concepts and theory. Follow the rules outlined here and you will be able to engage your nontechnical audience and perhaps extract some useful information from them along the way.

Figure 2-17 displays a sample model that observes Barker's positional rules, whereby the reference entities are located to the right of the associated transactional entities, and all of the *transaction-type* entities (on the *many* side of crow's feet) are located either above or to the left of the reference entities. Don't worry about the fine details of this model right now; these will be taken up in later chapters.

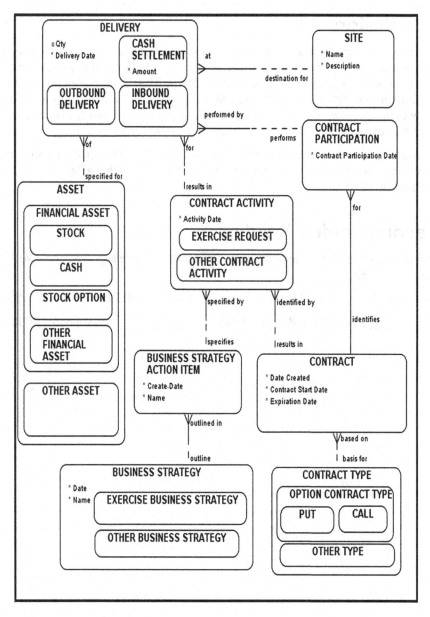

Figure 2-17. Example of Barker's positional conventions

Conclusion

Barker's CASE methodology provides a set of powerful data modeling techniques used and appreciated by modelers worldwide. If you discipline yourself to follow Barker's guidelines, your data models will become more user-friendly and less buggy, and you may find yourself engaging your audience more effectively than you have in the past. In addition to being crisper and clearer, Barker's methodology promotes well-articulated and better organized designs.

All the diagrams in this book are based on Barker's ideas. If this is your first introduction to Barker's CASE method, I urge you consult these Recommended Readings here.

Recommended Readings

Barker, Richard. *CASE Method: Entity Relationship Modelling.* Addison-Wesley Longman, 1990.

Hay, David C. *Data Model Patterns: Conventions of Thought.* Dorset House, 1995.

_____. *Data Model Patterns: A Metadata Map.* Morgan Kaufmann, 2006.

Financial Contracts

Each problem that I solved became a rule, which served afterwards to solve other problems.

—René Descartes, *Le Discours de la Méthode*

To provide a foundation for the rest of this book, this chapter defines the terminology and discusses the basics of financial contracts.

What Is a Contract?

A *contract* is a binding agreement between two or more parties to exchange specified goods or services on specified terms. At least two parties must be engaged if there is to be a valid contract: a party that proposes something and a party that accepts that something (Figure 3-1). An agreement to sell and buy a particular product or service at a certain point in time and at a particular price is an example of a simple contract. Besides the offeror and the offeree, additional parties may participate in a given contract in various capacities, such as joint offerees, agents, receivers, referenced subsidiaries, and executors. For instance, one party may draft a particular contract and another party may supervise it. Your organization will identify the participants it wants to store and maintain well in advance, most likely based on the roles these parties play in the underlying contract.

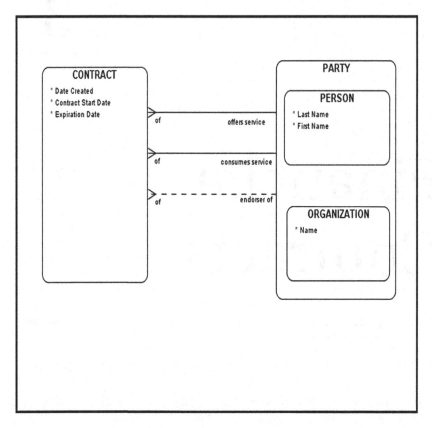

Figure 3-1. Model of a basic contract

A party may play multiple roles in any given contract. The CONTRACT entity, the way it is modeled in Figure 3-1, must be associated with at least two other PARTIES (identified by the "offers service" and "consumes service" relationships), with the "endorser of" relationship being optional. One limitation of this model is immediately obvious: it cannot be easily extended in terms of role specification. For instance, a PARTY may play the role of a "legal advisor" or a "contract draftee" for the underlying CONTRACT, and the model may need to account for this. Remember that a contract (especially a financial one) may contain a significant number of details; it is a legal document, and each aspect of it may need to be represented in the model. Faced with such a need, it is reasonable to consider extending (or widening) the CONTRACT entity by appending attributes to it, but this solution is not very elegant and is highly rigid. By resorting to this approach, we are limiting ourselves to extending our model only through a *data definition language* (DDL), which eventually might require us to alter our programming logic. Anyone who has attempted this approach will tell you that it is a nightmare for both project architects and code developers.

Another feature the plain vanilla model in Figure 3-1 lacks is the ability to create party roles dynamically. Your organization may identify a pool of roles they are interested in storing and maintaining. Even if this pool is approved by upper management, there is no guarantee that the list won't be altered. One option would be to hard code these party roles; another option would be to introduce a new entity, a ROLE TYPE, resulting in an elegant and creative solution to the problem (Figure 3-2).

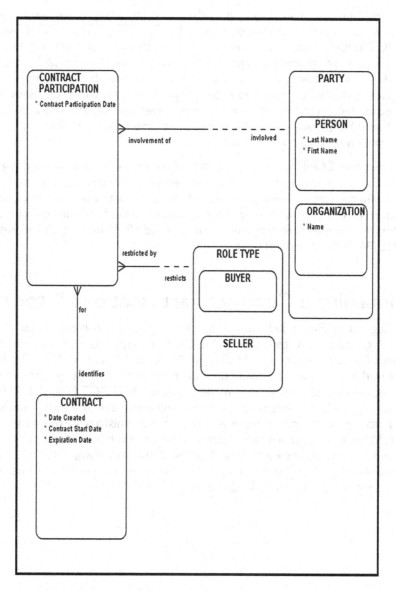

Figure 3-2. Model of contract participation

Note the solid (mandatory) relationship line between the CONTRACT and CONTRACT PARTICIPATION. Typically, you should approach mandatory-on-both-ends relationships (including one-to-many relationships) with caution. This doesn't mean that such configurations don't exist or that they should always be avoided. Mandatory-on-both-ends relationships do exist, albeit not very often, and they serve a particular purpose and emphasize a unique business rule.

In our example, the mandatory-on-both-ends relationship emphasizes a business rule which states that the entries in the CONTRACT and CONTRACT PARTICIPATION entities must be populated within the same transaction. For instance, your programming logic will have to ensure that for each contract you have at least two contract participants, with one playing the buyer and one playing the seller role. Note that a given contract may be associated with other roles (and not solely those of buyer and seller), and a business rule should be developed that clearly specifies the role types that are critical within the context of a given contract.

Note that the CONTRACT PARTICIPATION entity has not been designed to store and maintain historical data. As mentioned previously, modelers are often obligated (from a legal perspective) to maintain and keep track of every alteration to the contract's data. To maintain an accurate contract participation history, I suggest creating a new entity called HISTORICAL CONTRACT PARTICIPATION, discussed next.

Maintaining a Contract Participation History

The diagram in Figure 3-3 models a solution to the problem posed in the preceding section: how to create and maintain a proper contract participation history. The purpose of the HISTORICAL CONTRACT PARTICIPATION entity in this example is to maintain and store all of the changes (insertions, updates, and deletions) that were made to the CONTRACT PARTICIPATION records. Typically, in a large database one will find a set of "HIST_" prefixed tables that are intended to store and maintain the history of the underlying tables. Whenever a record gets altered in the source table, a database trigger fires and propagates the necessary changes to the underlying "HIST_" tables. A *database trigger* is a piece of code that is attached to a table and executed in response to certain predefined events.

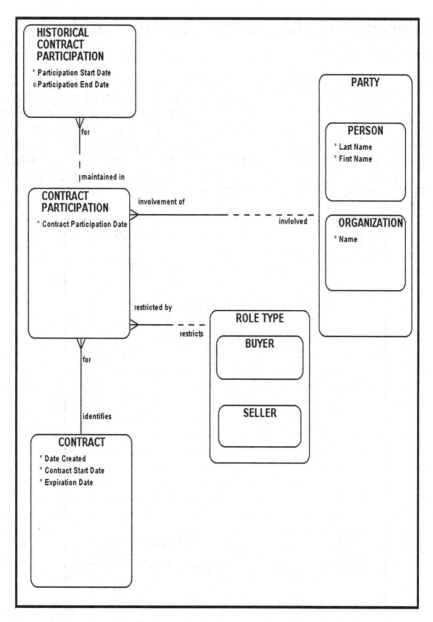

Figure 3-3. Example of a properly maintained contract participation history

Differentiating between a Contract and a Contract Type

The model in Figure 3-4 introduces another entity called a CONTRACT TYPE. A CONTRACT TYPE represents a catalog or blueprint of all available contracts. A CONTRACT, on the other hand, represents a legal entity—a physical embodiment of a contract type—to which at least two parties have agreed and signed on a particular date. If we adopt the *object-oriented* (OO) terminology, we say that a CONTRACT TYPE A (a subtype of a CONTRACT TYPE) is a base class that can be instantiated. An instance of a CONTRACT TYPE A base class is the actual CONTRACT.

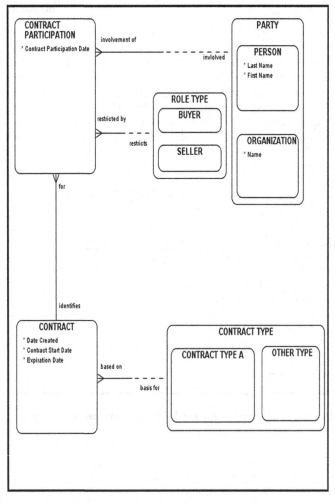

Figure 3-4. Differentiating between a contract and a contract type

Another important concept that often confuses novice modelers is the notion that a given contract type implicitly embeds within it a discrete set of business rules. These underlying business rules are usually quite familiar to the subject matter experts, and our job as modelers is often to explicitly associate a given contract with a proper contract type. For instance, assume that a financial company will deal with two contract types: contract types A and B. Contract type A requires participants to exchange physical assets up front; contract type B is the more typical type, whereby which physical assets are only exchanged on contract expiration. As you can see, associating a given contract with the wrong contract type will result in multiple inconsistencies and ambiguities. Imagine what would happen if a particular contract is linked to the wrong contract type (for the sake of our example, let's say contract type A). A relationship between our example contract and contract type A would imply that the underlying physical assets are to be exchanged at the start of the contract. However, this is clearly wrong, and our resulting data model would only further confuse our subject matter experts. A tarnished data model immediately loses credibility and suffers the consequences of being branded irrelevant. Learn to correctly associate your model types with the physical embodiment of those types and you will protect yourself from these unnecessary ambiguities and misunderstandings.

Assets and Asset Types

The core difference between an asset and an asset type is similar to the difference between a contract and contract type (see Figure 3-5). An *asset type* is a blueprint—something that exists only on paper, which you cannot hold or touch. An *asset*, on the other hand, is something that holds a value and you can physically hold and touch. This distinction between an asset and asset type is especially crucial within the context of a financial contract. The important thing to remember is this: if you don't hold it, you don't own it. Unfortunately, some business people treat assets and asset types as one and the same and learn the difference the hard way. Train yourself to separate and differentiate between paper (an asset type) and physical assets, and model them accordingly.

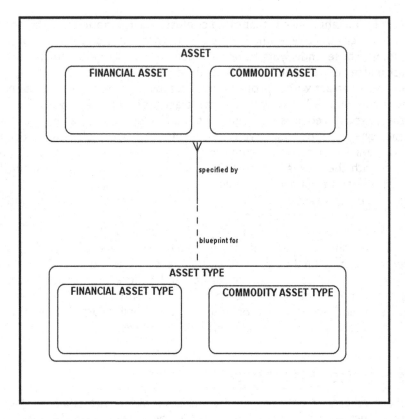

Figure 3-5. Model of asset and asset type

The Importance of Ownership Recognition

Things that are owned with a recognized level of ownership are considered assets. Examples of assets include stocks and precious metals held in an individual's possession. Even though you may have a printout confirming a level of ownership, a stock certificate or a grant of deed are legally binding indications of ownership. Paper assets are things that you don't own, at least not in this sense.

For instance, consider a *debt coupon*. Here, someone has borrowed a physical asset (in this case, cash) and made a promise to return payment via a debt coupon (a paper asset, at this point). Unfortunately, a debt coupon is just a piece of paper that confirms a debt. Try taking it to a grocery store and offering it to a store clerk in exchange for groceries. In all likelihood, the sales clerk may not even understand what you are offering. You can bet that he will refuse to let you leave with your groceries. The debt coupon will remain yours to deal with until your counterparty pays back the owed amount.

A *stock option* is another example of an asset that points to a paper asset. An option is the paper record of a promise to allow the bearer to buy a stock at some point in the future (a paper asset) at a specific price. Unless you exercise your right to buy the specified stock, you don't own the stock and it cannot be counted toward a portfolio of physical assets.

These examples demonstrate the notion that physical assets and asset types are different and shouldn't be confused. Each performs a separate function and should be used in a proper context. In most cases (there are a few exceptions, of course), financial contracts will point to paper assets (or asset types) to signify that the contractually promised things are to be viewed as promises.

Modeling Contract Asset Allocations

The diagram in Figure 3-6 models a CONTRACT ASSET ALLOCATION entity and the associated relationships. As you can see, a physical asset is not even displayed in the starter data model. The reason for this is that each asset listed in the underlying financial contract is a paper asset (or an asset type). Paper assets refer to things that can be held but are held by someone else. The primary on the contract merely has a claim to a promise that someone else has made. When someone promises to deliver a ton of aluminum in one month, the actual asset type under consideration is a paper asset (an aluminum asset type). As everybody knows, promises are meant to be broken. Don't treat contractually promised things as assets, because they are paper assets (or asset types). Only once your counterparty delivers the assets will those assets be counted toward (or against) a physical asset inventory.

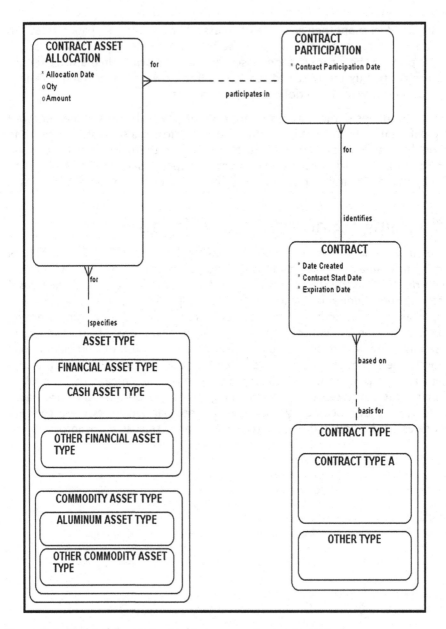

Figure 3-6. Model of the relationships between contract and asset type

A CONTRACT ASSET ALLOCATION specifies which paper assets each PARTY is responsible for within the context of the financial CONTRACT. Financial contracts typically involve two assets. For example, if an investor promises a delivery of copper in exchange for a specific amount of cash, two asset types come into play: a copper asset type and a cash asset type. This brings us to an interesting point: a financial contract can be viewed as a mechanism that transforms, upon completion of delivery, one asset into another. In the copper-for-cash example, one asset (cash) is transformed on completion of the delivery into another (copper). Consider a hypothetical example of how a CONTRACT ASSET ALLOCATION is used.

Example   Assume that today is January 1, 2014. Investor A signs a contract with investor B and agrees to purchase 10 tons of aluminum for US$10,000 on July 1, 2014. The result is a very simple contract involving two parties—investor A and investor B—with a contract expiration date of July 1, 2014. Note that the contract in question involves two asset types: a CASH ASSET TYPE (for the sake of simplicity we assume here that investor A will pay with cash) and an ALUMINUM ASSET TYPE. Inasmuch as a contract is a promise, its underlying assets should be treated as paper assets. Thus, we need to store two records in the CONTRACT ASSET ALLOCATION: one associating investor A with the CASH ASSET TYPE (a subtype of the FINANCIAL asset type) and a set amount equal to $10,000; the other record will associate investor B with an ALUMINUM ASSET TYPE (a subtype of the COMMODITY ASSET TYPE) and set the quantity equal to 10 tons.

The model in Figure 3-6 provides no means of specifying units of measure (here, tons). The diagram in Figure 3-7 clarifies this issue and shows how to associate a UNIT OF MEASURE with a CONTRACT ASSET ALLOCATION. Note that the relationship between the CONTRACT ASSET ALLOCATION and the UNIT OF MEASURE is nonmandatory on both sides. This is done by design, because not every asset type will have a true unit of measure.

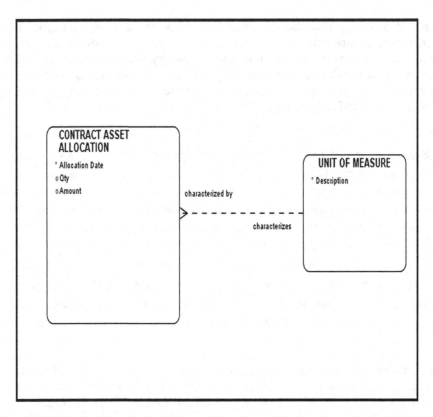

Figure 3-7. Model of the relationship between contract asset allocation and unit of measure

Once the two records are stored in the CONTRACT ASSET ALLOCATION, you can always return and reconstruct the terms of your contract to list all of the involved parties and their corresponding roles, the asset types involved, and the parties responsible for them.

Contract Structure and Contract Type Structure

Often, your requirements may call for the creation of a *complex contract*—one that is made up of other contracts. For instance, the underlying business strategy may involve entering into one contract at time T1, then entering into another contract at time T2, and finally entering into a third contract to offset the first two contracts at time T3. Sound complicated? They can be, but these brain-teasing data structures (Figure 3-8) occur quite frequently in practice; it would be wise to familiarize yourself with them at this early stage. One way of interpreting the meaning of the CONTRACT TYPE STRUCTURE entity is to think of the numerous ways that various contract types can be combined with one another to create something more complicated than the basic contract type would allow. The ability to combine various physical contracts into a well-defined pattern leads to a CONTRACT STRUCTURE, which may be specified by a CONTRACT TYPE STRUCTURE.

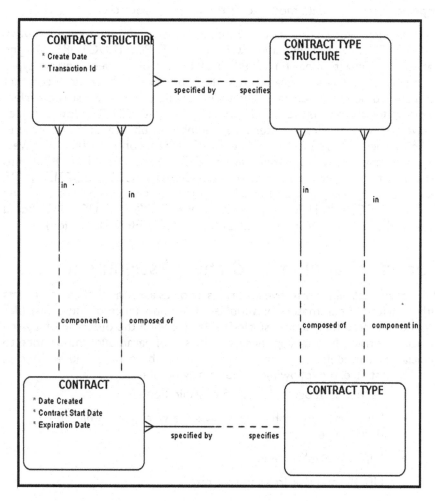

Figure 3-8. Contract structure and contract type structure

In financial engineering, a given financial contract is often combined and packaged with other contracts to create a financial instrument with a specific payoff function. This combination makes the underlying business rules more complex. However, once you are familiar with the basic building blocks and understand the meanings of these complex structures, you will be able to apply your knowledge without confusion or hesitation.

According to your model, the CONTRACT STRUCTURE may or may not depend on the CONTRACT TYPE STRUCTURE. You can, in fact, make this relationship mandatory to enforce the rule that each CONTRACT STRUCTURE must be specified by one and only one CONTRACT TYPE STRUCTURE. Typically, your business requirements will guide you on how to shape your resulting data model to fit the needs of your client.

The following hypothetical example will help clarify the difference between CONTRACT STRUCTURE and CONTRACT TYPE STRUCTURE. Imagine that your organization has published an official list of allowed contract types and a corresponding specification that describes exactly how these contract types should be combined, including their specific order. This list is a perfect candidate for storage in the CONTRACT TYPE STRUCTURE. Now consider an investor who decides to enter into a number of physical contracts to create some specific payoff function. The list of physical contracts that our investor enters into should be stored in the CONTRACT STRUCTURE. If this investor is to be forced to consult with the CONTRACT TYPE STRUCTURE data before entering into a physical contract, the relationship between the CONTRACT STRUCTURE and the CONTRACT TYPE STRUCTURE should be altered to be mandatory (on the CONTRACT STRUCTURE side).

Contract Variables and Their Assignment

Quite often modeling derivative contracts involves associating those contracts with a variety of parameters or *variables*. The importance of these variables is immense; often they almost single-handedly decide the outcome of a given financial contract. Maintaining these variables is of paramount importance to financial data modelers, and their design should be approached with great care. For instance, the following variables may be of use:

- Particular geographic region precipitation level

- Particular geographic region average weekly, monthly, or daily temperature

- Implied volatility values

- LIBOR[1] and risk-free interest rate

You may be wondering why an investor would be interested in knowing temperature and precipitation levels. If the investor is involved in an agricultural contract, he or she will be very interested to know whether a drought is expected in a particular region and what percentage of his or her crop may be affected.

---

[1] The *London Interbank Offered Rate (LIBOR)* is the rate of interest at which one bank is prepared to deposit money into another bank.

As an alternative to hard coding these variables into the application code, the model depicted in Figure 3-9 solves this problem with a more elegant, dynamic approach.[2] The many-to-many relationship between a given CONTRACT and a VARIABLE is resolved with the help of a VARIABLE ASSIGNMENT intersection entity. Here we can dynamically specify the variables to be used to valuate our contract and determine its outcome.

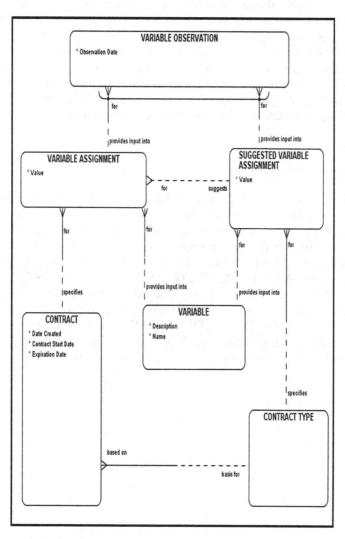

Figure 3-9. Modeling variables

---

[2]Figure 3-9 evokes David C. Hay's work on modeling variables in various industries set forth in his pioneering books on modeling patterns listed in the "Recommended Readings" section of this chapter.

A SUGGESTED VARIABLE ASSIGNMENT intersection entity resolves the many-to-many relationship between a VARIABLE and a CONTRACT TYPE. The purpose of this entity is to suggest variables that a given contract type might require. You can treat the entity as a suggestion because the relationship between the SUGGESTED VARIABLE ASSIGNMENT and the VARIABLE ASSIGNMENT is nonmandatory on both sides. Your requirements will direct you on how to model this relationship. If necessary, you may make this relationship a mandatory one to enforce the business rule that each variable assignment must be suggested by a suggested variable assignment. A VARIABLE OBSERVATION entity stores the actual variable observations recorded at a specific date and time. The two relationships coming out of the VARIABLE OBSERVATION are mutually exclusive, as you may only physically observe either a contract-assigned variable (via a VARIABLE ASSIGNMENT) or a variable specified via a SUGGESTED VARIABLE ASSIGNMENT.

Business Strategy

This section considers an entity called BUSINESS STRATEGY (see Figure 3-10). A *business strategy* outlines a set of actions directed toward maintaining a given company's competitive advantage. Alternatively it may be viewed as a method a company might use to improve its bottom line. Quite often, practitioners must model a business strategy within the context of a particular financial contract. A SETTLEMENT STRATEGY and a CONTRACT MARKET ASSESSMENT are two examples of business strategies. The set of action items required to execute a particular BUSINESS STRATEGY are outlined in the BUSINESS STRATEGY ACTION ITEMS. These rules often become a set of *standard operating procedures* (SOPs) that guide businesses on how to proceed and which steps to take under certain conditions.

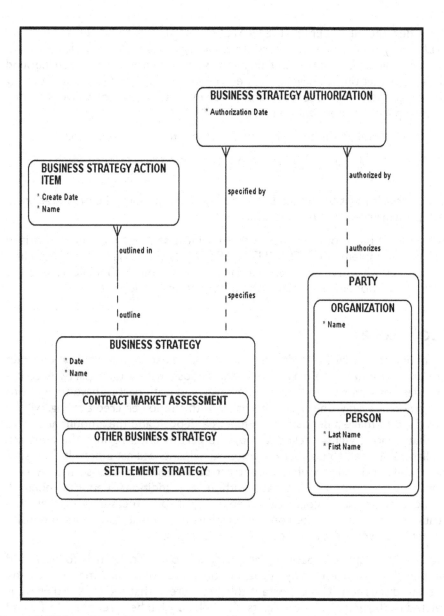

Figure 3-10. Introducing business strategy and business strategy action items

Consider the SETTLEMENT STRATEGY. BUSINESS STRATEGY ACTION ITEMS may outline the necessary steps an organization must perform to terminate a particular contract, including the steps required to accept an inbound delivery. Accepting a delivery is an extremely complicated process, requiring the cooperation of numerous parties. For instance, to accept delivery from a counterparty, an organization must:

- Arrange the transportation of assets to a final destination.
- Identify the individuals who are to be responsible for certain activities.

These details must be outlined well in advance to prepare the organization to accept deliveries from outside sources.

As a critical piece of every business, a business strategy must be authorized before it is implemented. The BUSINESS STRATEGY AUTHORIZATION lists the parties who have authorized a particular BUSINESS STRATEGY and the dates corresponding to when such authorizations took place.

Collateral

To minimize the risk of a default, parties participating in a financial contract are usually required to make a *collateral* deposit with a third party. A collateral deposit is not a requirement, however, and both parties have to agree to it. Sometimes only one party, the party with the lower credit rating, will be obligated to make a deposit. Who makes a deposit and the amount and form of that deposit will be negotiated by the parties entering into the contract. Collateral is used to protect contract participants against a default. The simplest collateral schema obliges contract participants to deposit money only once, on the contract start date, without any additional deposits required. A more complicated collateral schema may involve measuring market fluctuations and requiring the contract participants to make additional deposits, sometimes even daily, to reflect any market shifts.

Figure 3-11 depicts a basic collateral data model. To keep it focused and simple, this figure lists only those entities that contribute meaning to the current discussion. The important thing to note is that the COLLATERAL is related to the actual physical assets. The relationship between the PARTY and the COLLATERAL helps us identify any third party who might be temporarily holding any physical assets referenced in the contract. According to our model, the third party may be either a PERSON or an ORGANIZATION.

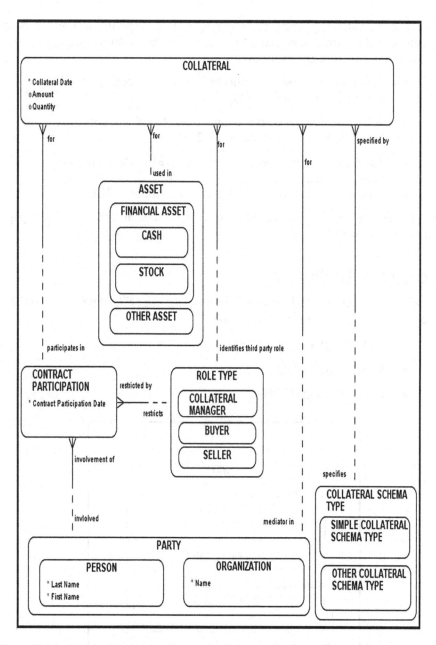

Figure 3-11. Model of forward contract collateral

Consider the following hypothetical example. Two companies, A and B, have agreed to enter into a financial contract and make collateral deposits. The terms of this contract are as follows:

- Company A agrees to purchase a ton of copper from company B for US$10,000.

- The contract start date is June 1, 2014, and the contract expiration date is December 1, 2014.

- Both companies agree to deposit US$10,000 each (the collateral deposit) with a third company, C, for the time period between June 1, 2014, and December 1, 2014.

In this case the simplest collateral schema is chosen, and the collateral payments are deposited only once.

Contract Delivery

Modeling contract delivery (Figure 3-12) involves the DELIVERY entity and its associated subtypes, including the following:

- OUTBOUND DELIVERY

- INBOUND DELIVERY

- CASH SETTLEMENT

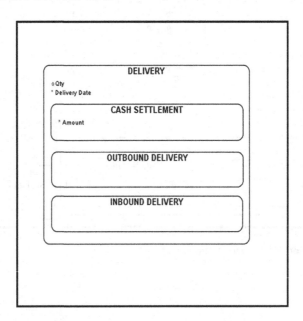

Figure 3-12. Subtyping delivery

Whenever one delivers an asset to fulfill a given contract (either fully or partially), one makes an *outbound delivery*. Whenever one receives an asset that fulfills (either fully or partially) a given contract, one accepts an *inbound delivery*. *Cash settlement* is another subtype of delivery that plays an important role in settling financial contracts. A large percentage of financial contracts can only be settled in cash. Note that in all of these cases (whether cash settlements or inbound/outbound deliveries), at least one physical asset is received.

The most important reason for subtyping the delivery entity is legal. The association of a given contract with a delivery subtype is pertinent when questions arise regarding the legality of certain delivery methods. All contracts, especially financial ones, may have legal repercussions. Models should reflect and enable reconstruction of every legal nuance, no matter how minor. Delivery subject area is a critical piece of the legal puzzle, and great care should be taken to describe and model it properly.

Another interesting aspect of the delivery subject area is the concept of *partial deliveries*. Partial deliveries occur when the buyer receives only a part of the agreed-upon quantity of items. For example, investor A might expect to receive 10 tons of aluminum bars by a certain date. The counterparty, investor B, may only be able to deliver nine tons of aluminum bars by that date. In most cases, investor A will hold off paying investor B until the full quantity (10 tons) has been delivered.

Your underlying business rule may allow for partial deliveries, in which case you may be called on to model them. The model in Figure 3-13 shows you how partial deliveries may be modeled by using what should by now be the familiar one-to-many recursive relationship. (Note that the CASH SETTLEMENT subtype from this model is removed to keep things simple.) The main reason partial deliveries are not that common in practice is that warehouse and transportation costs are high. Modern economic theory teaches that there's no such thing as a "free lunch" and someone always has to pick up the resulting tab (and most financial contract participants are reluctant to do so).

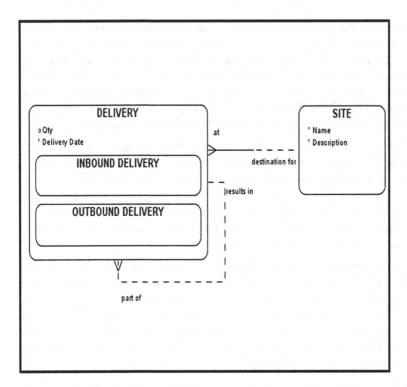

Figure 3-13. Modeling partial deliveries

Figure 3-14 models the contract's delivery subject area. (For clarity and simplicity, entities not related to the current discussion are not included in the figure.) Those activities executed on behalf of a given contract are stored in the CONTRACT ACTIVITY. These contract activities are specified by BUSINESS STRATEGY ACTION ITEMS, which in turn are identified by a BUSINESS STRATEGY. The SETTLEMENT STRATEGY, a subtype of the BUSINESS STRATEGY, is explicitly dedicated to dealing with the contract's settlement, and outlines the necessary steps to effectuate that settlement. SETTLEMENT RELATED ACTIVITY, a subtype of the CONTRACT ACTIVITY, groups together all of the settlement activities performed on behalf of the given CONTRACT.

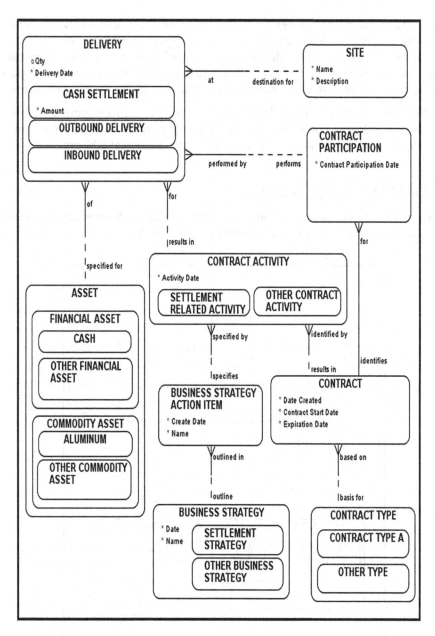

Figure 3-14. Contract delivery

SETTLEMENT RELATED ACTIVITIES may result in the actual DELIVERY of the physical assets. *Delivery*, within the context of a given contract, may mean a number of things. The most familiar example is when an exchange of assets takes place: one party delivers a ton of copper (an asset) and receives another asset in return (cash, for instance). Sometimes a given contract results in a cash settlement. Under a cash settlement, one party pays its counterparty a certain amount of cash based on the price difference between the amount agreed upon in the contract and asset's current market price (called the asset's spot price).

A SITE associated with a DELIVERY may be a physical address (thus specifying a delivery address). For example, when a party delivers corn to a particular warehouse, the SITE will identify its location (or a physical address).

Contract Regulations

A contract is a promise, and promises are often broken. A potential end result of a broken promise is a lengthy lawsuit (Figure 3-15).

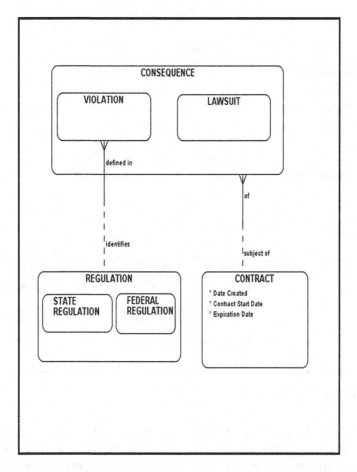

Figure 3-15. Modeling contract regulations

Consider the following scenario. Farmer A decides to purchase a cow from farmer B, and they sign a contract. Farmer A inspects farmer B's cattle and both farmers agree on a particular cow. Moreover, both farmers agree that the cow in question is sterile and settle in writing on the following terms:

- Method of payment (cash)

- Payment amount ($0.90 per pound)

- Delivery date

On the delivery date, farmer B realizes that the cow in question is actually pregnant and refuses to deliver it unless farmer A pays more for it. Farmer A refuses and files a lawsuit. Even though this is a relatively straightforward contract breach, the lawsuit outcome may not be so certain. For instance, if both farmers have subscribed in the contract to the mistaken material fact that the cow in question is barren, the court may consider this fact and side with farmer B.[3]

A contract may violate some type of REGULATION (subtyped into a STATE REGULATION or a FEDERAL REGULATION). For example, investor A may have violated federal law in the past and is now prohibited from entering into any type of financial contract until time T2. If this investor then enters into a financial contract before T2, the contract may be invalidated by federal regulators. You may be called on to model such situations (Figure 3-15).[4]

Conclusion

This chapter introduced basic concepts of financial contracts that the subsequent chapters on financial engineering data modeling will continually draw on.

Recommended Readings

Hay, David C. Data Model Patterns: Conventions of Thought. Dorset House, 1995.

_____. Data Model Patterns: A Metadata Map. Morgan Kaufmann, 2006.

---

[3]This hypothetical case is based on *Sherwood v. Walker* (66 Mich. 568, 33 N.W. 919, 1887), which was seminal in the evolution of the doctrine of *mutual mistake* in U.S. contract law.
[4]Figure 3-15 draws on David C. Hay's work on modeling patterns for "loss events" and regulations in the context of work orders set forth in his books on modeling patterns listed in the "Recommended Reading" section of this chapter.

Modeling Forward Contracts

I hope that posterity will judge me kindly, not only as to the things which I have explained, but also to those which I have intentionally omitted so as to leave to others the pleasure of discovery.

—René Descartes, *La Géométrie*

This chapter examines the specifics, mechanics, and terminology of a vastly popular contract type in the *over-the-counter* (OTC) market: the *forward contract* (or simply *forward*). The opening section defines a forward contract and describes its associated business rules.

Defining a Forward Contract

A *forward contract* is an agreement between two parties to buy or sell an asset for a certain price at a mutually agreed-upon future date. It is often contrasted with another relatively simple contact type, called a *spot contract*. A spot contract is an agreement between two parties to buy or sell an asset today.

The forward contract is a *nonstandardized contract*, meaning it is not traded on the main financial exchanges and is therefore considered riskier, in the sense that there is a greater chance than otherwise that one party might default on its obligation to buy or sell. Nonstandardized contracts typically involve large financial institutions that can absorb such a level of risk. Because forward contracts are nonstandard, they take a relatively long time to negotiate and execute. There are organizations that specialize in the creation of the various documents on which OTC contracts are based (including forward contracts). These documents are templates that may be tailored to the specific needs of the parties involved. Chapter 8 discusses these documents and their associated structure.

Forward Contract Specifications

A party that agrees to buy an asset at some point in the future takes a *long* position in a given forward contract. A party that agrees to sell an asset at some point in the future takes a *short* position in a given forward contract. A *spot price* is the price of a given asset right now. It is contrasted with a *forward price* (aka *delivery price*), which is a mutually agreed-upon price of an asset in the future.

Consider, for example, an investor who needs to pay back 1,000,000 GBP on January 1, 2015. Let's assume that today is January 1, 2014. This private investor has a hunch that the USD/GBP exchange rate may go up (thus, it will take more U.S. dollars to purchase British pounds). One strategy the investor might consider is to agree to an *offer rate* proposed by a bank and enter into a 12-month forward contract (Table 4-1). As a result, the investor agrees to purchase from the bank in one year 1,000,000 GBP for US$2,039,000. Because he has agreed to purchase a particular currency (pounds sterling), the private investor is holding a long position in the underlying forward contract. The bank, on the other hand, has agreed to sell 1,000,000 GBP for US$2,039,000 and is holding a short position in the underlying forward contract. The forward contract that the private investor and the bank have signed becomes a binding agreement which both parties have agreed to honor one year from the date of signature.

Note that the terms *bid* and *offer* in the Table 4-1 caption are prices from the standpoint of the financial institution that provides them. A bid is the price that the financial institution is prepared to pay to purchase a given asset. An offer is the financial institution's selling price.

Table 4-1. Bid/Offer Quotes

Spot Price	Bid	Offer
1 Month Forward Contract	2.0345	2.0351
6 Month Forward Contract	2.0312	2.0321
12 Month Forward Contract	2.031	2.039

An ASSET underlying a particular forward contract may be grouped into one of the following two categories: an INVESTMENT ASSET or a CONSUMPTION ASSET (Figure 4-1). The main purpose of the *consumption asset* is to keep business running smoothly—for example, a constant supply of natural gas to keep furnaces burning or machine oil to keep planes flying. Without the raw materials necessary to do its business, a company risks significant losses, work stoppages, and unpaid wages. An *investment asset*, on the other hand, is used for speculative purposes (such as stocks and bonds).

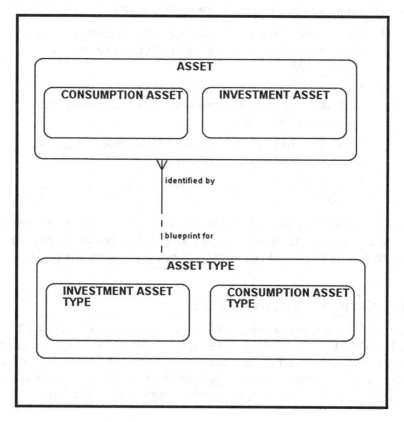

Figure 4-1. Consumption and investment assets/asset types

Reversing a position or canceling a forward contract is very difficult and one of the most significant shortcomings of the OTC market. Upon expiration, a forward contract results in one of the following outcomes:

1. Physical delivery of an asset

2. Cash settlement

3. Default of one of the parties

The section "Forward Contract Termination" discusses various strategies that investors might use to early terminate a forward contract to protect themselves from an unfavorable outcome.

The discussion in this chapter makes the following assumptions:

1. At least two parties participate in a given forward contract. In particular, one party holds a long position (the buyer) and its counterparty holds a short position (the seller).

2. Long and short positions are nontransferable.

3. Other parties may participate in a forward contract, and from a legal perspective it is important to store and maintain this data.

4. Assets involved in a forward contract have to be explicitly listed and explicitly associated with the parties that are responsible for them.

5. Forward contracts may generate multiple business activities that should be tracked for regulatory purposes.

6. Forward contracts result in delivery, cash settlement, or default.

Forward contracts are modeled in this chapter according to the specific subject areas and in a succession of steps. Diagrams modeled in this way are easier to read, manage, and interpret because they contain less noise.

Subtyping Contract Type

Figure 4-2 depicts (among other things) the subtyping of CONTRACT TYPE into FORWARD CONTRACT TYPE and OTHER TYPE. Your organization may deal with various other contract types (swaps and futures, for example). If this is the case, make sure that you add each of these contract types as subtypes in addition to your already existing forward contract type.

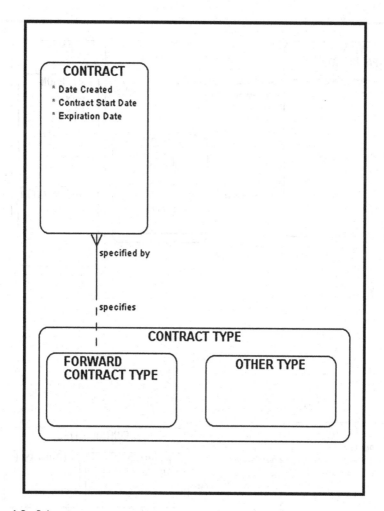

Figure 4-2. Subtyping contract type

Figure 4-2 exemplifies the basic principle of data model display management: keep things simple, focused, and concise. Keeping superfluous details out of your data models makes them easily understandable by your technical and nontechnical end users and makes your presentations more productive.

Forward Contract Data Modeling Basics

Figure 4-3 represents the first step in the construction of a forward contract's data model. The model at this point still lacks certain major pieces identified in the beginning of this chapter, which will be incrementally added in ensuing sections.

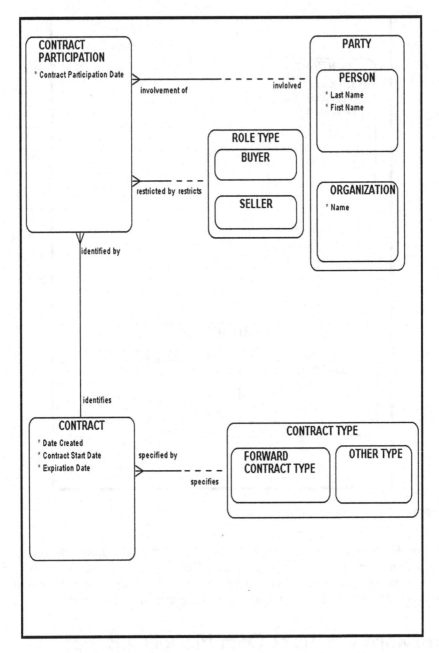

Figure 4-3. Forward contract's data modeling basics

The CONTRACT PARTICIPATION entity is designed to store and maintain an act of participation of a certain party or parties, along with the roles that they may play in a given forward contract. Your organization will help you identify these contract participation roles. Risk always plays a major role in financial contracts, and forward contracts are no exception. Trading in an unregulated and uncontrolled environment is risky because there is always a possibility of one party defaulting on a promise or contract. From a regulatory point of view, your organization may be obligated to keep track of each contract participant. In any event, at least two entity instances (or entries) in the CONTRACT PARTICIPATION entity will be mandatory; these are the parties who play the roles of BUYER and SELLER. Incidentally, this particular business rule cannot be shown directly in the diagram. Note the presence of the mandatory (on both sides) relationship between the CONTRACT and CONTRACT PARTICIPATION. Again, approach relationships that are mandatory on both sides with care. After all, relationships that are mandatory on both sides force us to answer a "chicken or egg" causality dilemma. Even though a true relationship that is mandatory on both sides occurs infrequently in practice, it does happen, and you have every right to question its validity. In our case, the mandatory relationship between the CONTRACT and the CONTRACT PARTICIPATION signifies that these entities should be populated as part of the same transaction. In other words, whenever you populate CONTRACT data, make sure to insert at least two records—namely, a BUYER and a SELLER——into the CONTRACT PARTICIPATION.

CONTRACT stores contract-specific information, such as contract start date, expiration dates, and contract create date. CONTRACT TYPE specifies a particular contract template, along with the corresponding business rules that a given contract implicitly inherits.

Most of its features and components of the Figure 4-3 data model are familiar because they were already discussed in Chapter 3. Many of the modeling pieces and concepts presented there recur throughout this book, because they supply models that incorporate the capacity to accommodate change. Hastily building models from scratch is anathema in most fields, especially in the realm of financial data modeling. Modeling patterns are designs that have been tested and approved by the general modeling community. They have been successfully deployed on multiple platforms and are generic enough to accommodate various changes. By recognizing a particular modeling pattern and applying it to solve a particular business problem, you will markedly enhance the overall quality of your design and improve your communication of it to end users because industry-approved design patterns are generally intuitive and simple to implement.

Associating Forward Contracts with Asset Types

Figure 4-3 lacks associations with asset types (or paper assets). This deficiency is remedied in the Figure 4-4 model.

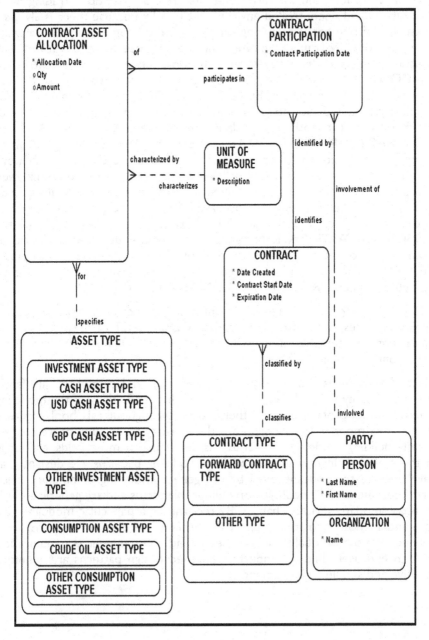

Figure 4-4. Forward contract and contract asset allocation

The purpose of the CONTRACT ASSET ALLOCATION entity is to keep track of which underlying ASSET TYPE each PARTY (implemented through CONTRACT PARTICIPATION) is responsible for within the context of a given CONTRACT. For example, assume that:

- Investor A agrees to purchase 100 barrels of crude oil from investor B for US$10,000,

- Contract start date is January 1, 2014, and

- Contract expiration date is July 1, 2014.

This particular forward contract involves two asset types: the CRUDE OIL ASSET TYPE (a CONSUMPTION ASSET TYPE subtype) and a CASH ASSET TYPE (an INVESTMENT ASSET TYPE subtype). The purpose of the CONTRACT ASSET ALLOCATION is to associate each contract participant (namely, the buyer and seller) with the appropriate ASSET TYPE, along with the corresponding amount and quantity (whichever is applicable), all performed within the context of a given forward contract.

Note that the Figure 4-4 diagram does not relate CONTRACT ASSET ALLOCATION to the physical assets. This is deliberate, because a contract represents a promise to deliver something, and a promise is only a promise. One party can always default on its outstanding obligations at any time. Only at the delivery stage can we shift our focus and begin discussing physical assets; until that time, we must concern ourselves with modeling the asset types.

The CONTRACT ASSET ALLOCATION is used to store the amount and quantity attributes. In the example, investor A is associated with a CASH ASSET TYPE (a subtype of the INVESTMENT ASSET TYPE) and the amount is set to $10,000. CASH ASSET TYPE may be further subtyped into USD CASH ASSET TYPE and GBP CASH ASSET TYPE to precisely define the amount. Investor B is associated with the CRUDE OIL ASSET TYPE (a subtype of the CONSUMPTION ASSET TYPE) and the quantity attribute is set equal to 100. Knowing that investor B is associated with the CRUDE OIL ASSET TYPE and the quantity attribute is set to 100 is not enough, however, to reconstruct the terms of our contract because we don't know the underlying unit of measure. This is where the UNIT OF MEASURE entity comes in because it helps us specify that the CRUDE OIL ASSET TYPE quantity is measured in barrels. We assume that both parties have precisely defined what the contract refers to when it says "oil barrel." In the United States and Canada, for example, an oil barrel is equivalent to 42 US gallons. To stay flexible, another option would be to specify the unit of measure in US gallons and convert the quantity from the number of barrels to the number of gallons (100 x 42). Yet another option would be to adopt the metric system and specify the unit of measure as liters.

Note that the relationship between the UNIT OF MEASURE and the CONTRACT ASSET ALLOCATION is nonmandatory on both sides. This is by design because the UNIT OF MEASURE specification (within the context of the CONTRACT ASSET ALLOCATION) may not be applicable; it depends on the nature of the underlying ASSET TYPE.

If you closely inspect and analyze our starter data model, you should notice that we can easily reconstruct the nature of our contract to determine which ASSET TYPE each PARTY is responsible for, along with the associated quantity and amount attributes.

Forward Contracts and Variable Assignment

To properly model forward contracts, we need to account for the variables that play a role in deciding the outcome of those contracts—such as currency conversion rates, LIBOR rates, risk-free rates, and time to expiration. In addition to assigning variables, we should be able to valuate our forward contract at any particular point in time.

Figure 4-5 models variables within the context of a given contract. The SUGGESTED VARIABLE ASSIGNMENT is an intersection entity that resolves the many-to-many relationship between the VARIABLES and the CONTRACT TYPE. The SUGGESTED VARIABLE ASSIGNMENT entity is something that maintains an organizationally suggested, generic list of variables that are typically used in the context of a particular CONTRACT TYPE. Some of these variables are used to valuate the given CONTRACT. For instance, various interest rates and currency conversion rates are candidates for storage and maintenance in your model as variables. Later chapters will explore other methods for storing these items.

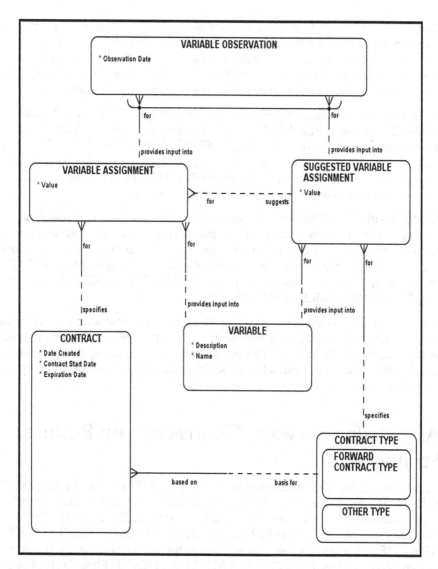

Figure 4-5. Forward contract and variable assignment

VARIABLE ASSIGNMENT, on the other hand, models the association between the VARIABLES and the CONTRACT. Variables specified via the SUGGESTED VARIABLE ASSIGNMENT may differ from the variables actually assigned to a particular CONTRACT. For instance, your organization may identify a generic set of market variables that a particular CONTRACT TYPE should store and maintain. However, in special cases (particularly when dealing with nonstandard contracts) an organization may be interested in maintaining a set of market variables specific to a particular CONTRACT. For example, if you are dealing with a forward contract to purchase corn, you may be interested in maintaining a particular region's temperature; one way you may do so is with the use of contract-specific variables. Moreover, your plain vanilla forward contract may require you to store and maintain the implied asset volatility, and you should be able to accommodate such a request with relative ease.

Note that the relationship between the VARIABLE ASSIGNMENT and the SUGGESTED VARIABLE ASSIGNMENT is nonmandatory on both sides. In other words, in our model the SUGGESTED VARIABLE ASSIGNMENT may "suggest" the VARIABLE ASSIGNMENT. You may have to alter this and make the relationship mandatory (on the VARIABLE ASSIGNMENT side). Typically, your requirements will guide you on how to proceed.

The VARIABLE OBSERVATION entity stores the results of the actual, physical observations performed on the variables in question: their value and the corresponding date and time when a particular observation is made. Note the presence of the exclusivity arc around the VARIABLE OBSERVATION entity, suggesting that it may store either the VARIABLE ASSIGNMENT or the SUGGESTED VARIABLE ASSIGNMENT, but not both.

The job of a financial engineer is to take these market variables, plug them into various statistical models, and use them to valuate a given forward contract at a particular point in time. The actual process of applying these variables to various mathematical models will be described separately for you by your process architects.

Associating Forward Contracts with Business Strategies

Figure 4-6 models the association between a CONTRACT and a BUSINESS STRATEGY. As discussed in Chapter 3, a BUSINESS STRATEGY classifies things that are of importance to the organization. BUSINESS STRATEGY is the entity where the SETTLEMENT STRATEGY and CONTRACT MARKET ASSESSMENTS are classified; action items required to execute a given strategy are recorded as BUSINESS STRATEGY ACTION ITEMS. CONTRACT ACTIVITY maintains the various BUSINESS STRATEGY ACTION ITEMS performed within the context of a given forward contract. Some of the CONTRACT ACTIVITIES, subtyped into SETTLEMENT RELATED ACTIVITIES, will lead to physical delivery.

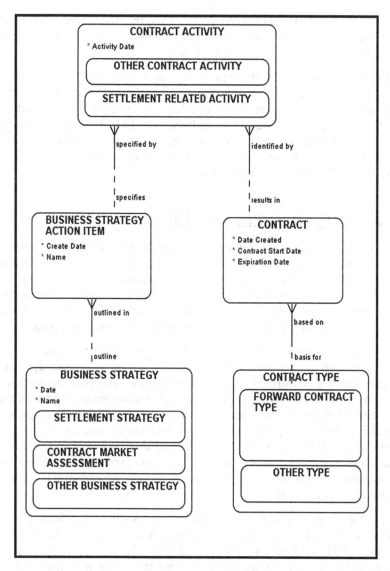

Figure 4-6. Associating forward contracts with business strategies

This section examines the SETTLEMENT STRATEGY subtype of the BUSINESS STRATEGY. Consider an investor who expects to receive 50,000 pounds of live cattle at US$0.96 per pound. Upon forward contract termination, the investor's counterparty will deliver the cattle to a mutually agreed-upon warehouse. Once the delivery is complete, the investor will look for methods to transport the cattle from the warehouse to the final destination. Any transport delays would likely result in punishing warehousing fees. In addition, once the investor accepts an inbound delivery of livestock, he is also responsible for its feeding. As you can see from this simple hypothetical case, there are numerous organizationally defined action items that must be executed to fulfill a given settlement strategy.

In general, the settlement strategy is a complicated mechanism with many moving parts, where one activity depends on the successful completion of other, well-planned activities. Any deviation from the plan will probably cost both time and money. The actual BUSINESS STRATEGY ACTION ITEMS that were implemented to meet the contract's SETTLEMENT STRATEGY are stored in the CONTRACT ACTIVITY, grouped under the SETTLEMENT RELATED ACTIVITIES (see Figure 4-6).

Forward Contracts and Delivery

A forward contract results either in a physical delivery or cash settlement (a positive outcome) or in a default (a negative outcome, typically leading to various lawsuits). In this section we model a positive outcome: when a given forward contract results in physical delivery. This section discusses and models the delivery mechanism linked to a financial asset. The delivery mechanism behind commodities is more complicated and is discussed in Chapter 5.

The definition of a consumption asset poses certain challenges due to significant variation in the quality parameters of the named asset. Special care is usually taken in contracts to precisely identify each publicly traded consumption asset to remove the possibility of misunderstanding or confusion at the time of delivery. For instance, a particular corn contract might specify a specific protein content range a buyer expects to receive. If the protein content of the delivered asset falls outside of this approved range, a few different things might occur. For instance, the product marked for delivery might be disqualified, or the resulting contract price might be reduced to reflect the reduced protein content.

Figure 4-7 gives you a good idea of how deliveries can be modeled within the context of forward contracts. As discussed in Chapter 3, DELIVERY is subtyped into OUTBOUND and INBOUND DELIVERIES. This subtyping allows us to explicitly track the type of delivery, what exactly was delivered, when, and by whom. It is important to keep track of exactly what each party under a given contract delivers, for both legal and regulatory purposes. Don't make the mistake of simply viewing delivery as the process of receiving something and paying (cash) for it—this is too simplistic. Delivery should instead be viewed as a type of asset transformation, in which one physical asset (cash) is transformed into another physical asset (gold, platinum, crude oil, etc.). There are numerous reasons for this asset transformation, including convenience and necessity. For instance, a factory plant might depend on a constant supply of crude oil; thus, it would be essential for the business to make sure that crude oil is in constant supply. In a case like this, the exchange of crude oil for cash would be done out of necessity. Note that according to our model, delivery is related to the physical assets, not to paper assets (or asset types). This is done by design. During the delivery phase, investors exchange physical assets and not paper assets. Once delivery is complete, you may add or subtract these assets to or from your physical asset inventory.

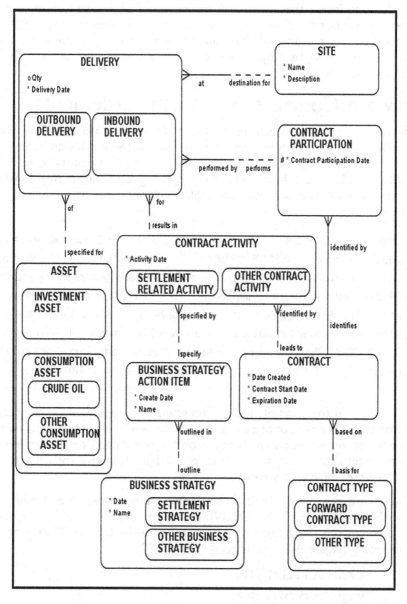

Figure 4-7. Modeling forward contract delivery

Have you noticed that this delivery model can accommodate partial deliveries, depending on your primary key selection? For instance, this model allows you to specify that investor A has delivered 100 barrels of crude oil to site A on a specific day, and 200 barrels of crude oil to site B on a different day. The 300 delivered barrels of crude oil satisfies a given contract (assuming that this contract was for 300 barrels of crude oil), which may be fine unless investor B objects and insists that investor A deliver them all to one location. Partial deliveries may not be allowed due to the excessive warehousing and transportation costs. Your underlying business requirements will guide you on how to proceed and will play a significant role in your primary key determination

Forward Contracts and Cash Settlements

A forward contract may result in a cash settlement in those situations where it becomes impractical to deliver the underlying asset. For instance, an OTC forward contract may involve the S&P 500 and entail one party delivering a portfolio of 500 stocks. In a situation like this, a given contract might instead be settled in cash. A hypothetical example to clarify the issue.

Example   Investor A enters into a forward contract to purchase one Treasury bill (T-bill, a paper asset) 60 days from now for US$1,000. Investor A takes a long position in the underlying forward contract. Investor B promises to sell one T-bill and is taking a short position in the underlying contract. If, on the settlement date, the price of the T-bill turns out to be $1,020, investor B may agree with investor A to settle the underlying contract in cash by delivering him $20 (a physical asset at this point). This particular forward contract has a *positive value* of $20 for investor A. If, on the other hand, the price of the T-bill on the settlement date turned out to be $990, investor A would have to pay $10 to investor B. In this case, a forward contract would have a *negative value* of $10 for investor A.

The behavior in this example may be generalized as follows. If, on the settlement date, the asset's spot price is above the forward price, an investor with a long position would receive payment. If, on the other hand, on the settlement date the asset's spot price is below the forward price, an investor with a short position would receive payment.

To model a forward contract cash settlement subject area, one should treat the CASH SETTLEMENT as a DELIVERY subtype. As discussed in Chapter 3, to implement this designation, you must subtype the DELIVERY into one of the following (Figure 4-8, reproducing Figure 3-12):

- CASH SETTLEMENT
- INBOUND DELIVERY
- OUTBOUND DELIVERY

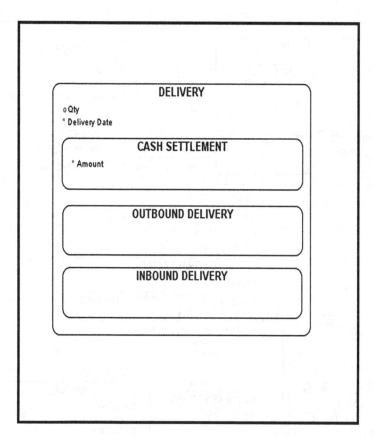

Figure 4-8. Delivery and cash settlement

Figure 4-9 depicts how a forward contract cash settlement mechanism may be modeled. This model is similar to the one depicted in Figure 4-7, where we modeled a forward contract's delivery subject area. Note the presence of the mandatory relationship between the DELIVERY entity and the SITE (mandatory on the DELIVERY side). This particular relationship enforces the business rule that the CASH SETTLEMENT should be associated with a specific SITE.

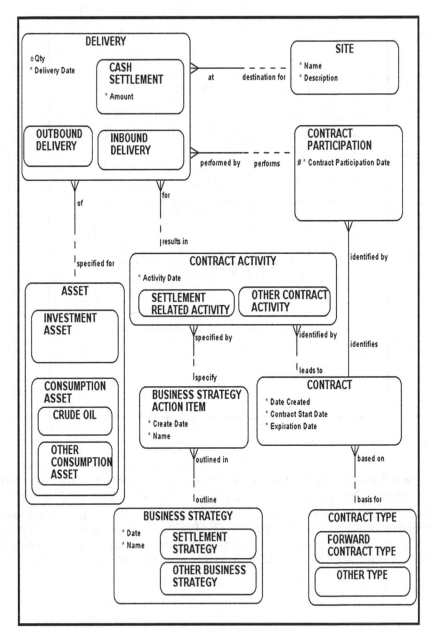

Figure 4-9. Forward contract cash settlement

Offsetting Forward Contracts

An investor can offset the risk of a forward contract by simultaneously entering into two forward contracts: one to sell an asset type, and the other to buy the same asset type (for instance, a foreign currency).

Consider an example: investor A enters into a forward contract that begins in one month (time T1) and lasts for one year (contract expiration date T2) to buy British pounds sterling (GBP) for a certain price (S1). At the same time the same investor enters into another forward contract, where the contract start date is T1 and the contract expiration date is T2, to sell British pounds sterling (GBP) for a certain price (S2). Cases like these occur frequently in practice, so it is important to learn how to model them.

The Figure 4-10 diagram keeps track of the overall contract strategy while ensuring that the modeler can easily track any CONTRACT dependencies and identify a group of related contracts (achieved through the CLASSIFICATION TYPE). Depending on your business requirements, you most likely will be asked to trace various contract dependencies and generate various historical data reports. The model, depicted in Figure 4-10, can easily accommodate requests like these. The CLASSIFICATION TYPE entity will be discussed further in subsequent chapters. Note the presence of the transaction ID attribute (a CONTRACT STRUCTURE entity). Its purpose is to link all related contracts together that are part of the same classification type.

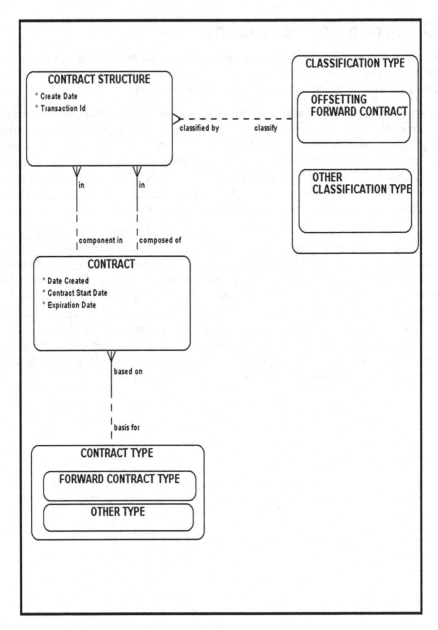

Figure 4-10. Maintaining contract dependency

Figure 4-11 presents a simpler variation on the structure depicted in Figure 4-10 that will allow you to keep track of various dependencies between several CONTRACTS by modeling contract dependency using a simple hierarchy. Before putting this model to use, however, make sure you are aware of its limitations. The structure implemented in Figure 4-10 (using the many-to-many recursive relationship) will give you a far better level of flexibility than what can be obtained with a simple hierarchy (as with Figure 4-11). I recommend that you keep your options open and, when the time comes, be ready to present multiple solutions to the same problem.

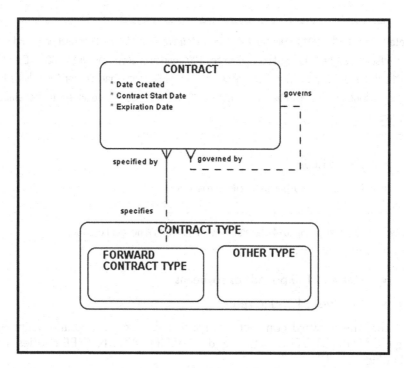

Figure 4-11. Maintaining contract dependency using a simple hierarchy

Forward Contract Termination

The main assumption behind forward contracts is that contract participants will retain their positions until the completion of the contract when completion delivery is made, payments are received, and the given contract is successfully closed. However, there are situations when one party would like to close out his or her position prior to contract termination. In cases like this, that party is taking an opposite position in a forward contract with the same underlying asset type and a similar expiration date. The forward price, however, will probably be different. An example will serve to illustrate this type of situation.

■ **Example**   Investor A enters into a soybean forward contract on the following terms:

- Starts on June 1, 2014
- Terminates on December 1, 2014
- The agreed-on quantity is 100 pounds
- Forward price is US$1,000

■ **Note**   On June 15, 2014, investor A decides to terminate this forward contract early and enters into an offsetting soybean forward contract to sell 100 pounds of soybeans for $1,100 on December 15, 2014. If you carefully analyze these transactions, you will realize that investor A simply limits his losses by locking in the December soybean price. If everything goes as planned, on December 1, 2014, investor A:

- Pays $1,000
- Obtains 100 pounds of soybeans

■ **Note**   On December 15, 2014, the same investor A (with a net gain of $100):

- Delivers 100 pounds of soybeans
- Receives $1,100 in return

Note that the forward contract termination can be tracked and maintained using CONTRACT STRUCTURE and CLASSIFICATION TYPE entities modeled in Figure 4-10.

Lawsuits and Violations

There will always a fear on the part of your end user that a party to the contract may need to default on his or her contractual obligation. Typically, the consequences of this default will be a lengthy lawsuit. Aside from lawsuits, a given contract may also be the subject of various REGULATIONS (FEDERAL REGULATIONS and STATE REGULATIONS). The Figure 4-12 diagram depicts how the CONSEQUENCE entity may be modeled.

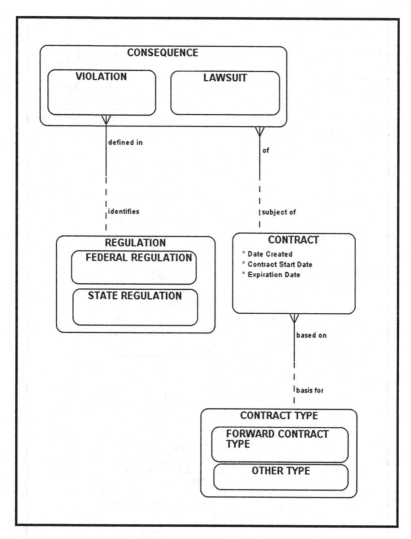

Figure 4-12. Modeling lawsuits and violations

In the Figure 4-12 model, the CONSEQUENCES are tracked on a CONTRACT level. You are always free to fine-tune this model and track the CONSEQUENCES on a CONTRACT ACTIVITY level. Indeed, sometimes it's not the contract itself but the actions performed on behalf of a given contract (represented by the CONTRACT ACTIVITY) that could be the subject of a lawsuit. The Figure 4-13 diagram extends the original "lawsuits and violations" model by relating CONSEQUENCE to CONTRACT ACTIVITY. Please note that the relationship between CONSEQUENCE and CONTRACT ACTIVITY is nonmandatory on both sides.

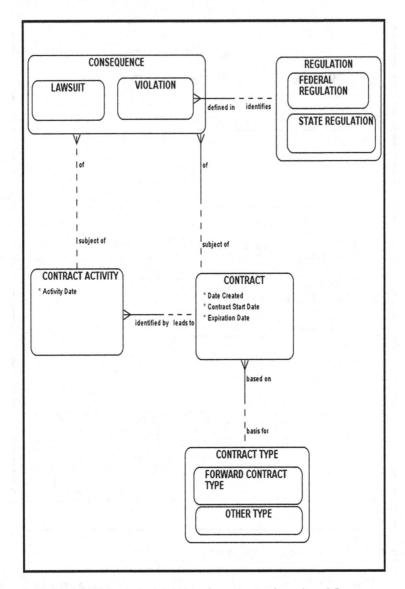

Figure 4-13. Modeling lawsuits and violations (a more complicated model)

Conclusion

This chapter introduced you to the complex world of forward contracts by discussing and modeling various business requirements ranging from forward contract delivery to forward contract consequences. The core building blocks used in this chapter were constructed and discussed in the previous chapters. This chapter focused on implementation, identifying a set of business rules, and creating various starter models by following those rules. After all, a contract is a contract, and once you know how to model it, you should be able to create a good starter model for any basic type. Once your starter model is complete, use your business rules to shape and mold it as required. Accommodate future changes preemptively through generalization, and don't sacrifice robustness and stability for ease of programming; you'll seldom be happy with the outcome.

Modeling Futures Contracts

When it is not in our power to follow what is true, we ought to follow what is most probable.

—René Descartes, *Le Discours de la Méthode*

Most of the modeling principles we learned in the last chapter are applicable to the subject of this chapter: *futures contracts* (aka *futures*). Futures share many features with forward contracts, but a fundamental difference between them is how each one approaches the risk factor. Forward contracts are risky, with the shadow of a default always looming. Futures contracts, on the other hand, are deemed to be less risky because they are traded on exchanges. Exchange-imposed rules buffer investors against some of the risk because they make default events less likely. Every major exchange has implemented a set of intricate rules that all concerned parties must follow and obey. Moreover, each exchange's enforcement of these rules guarantees that a contract has a good chance of being honored by each contract participant.

The following is a list of prominent exchanges where futures contracts are regularly traded: the *Chicago Board of Trade* (CBOT, www.cbot.com), *Chicago Board Options Exchange* (CBOE, www.cboe.com), *New York Stock Exchange* (NYSE, www.nyse.com), and *Chicago Mercantile Exchange* (CME, www.cme.com). A futures contract's underlying asset is either a commodity (pork bellies, crude oil, copper, etc.) or a financial asset (stocks, Treasury bonds, and so forth). Table 5-1 lists hypothetical grain futures quotes in the form provided by the CBOE.

Table 5-1. CBOE Grain Futures Quotes (Hypothetical)

Symbol	Contract	Month	Time	Last	Open	High	Low
S N3	SOYBEANS (OPEN OUTCRY)	SEPT13	18:44:08	1547	1534	1543	1527
ZS N3	SOYBEANS	SEPT13	18:41:02	1547	1530	1542	1526
SM N3	SOYBEAN MEAL (OPEN OUTCRY)	SEPT13	18:38:56	450	443	461	440
ZM N3	SOYMEAN MEAL	SEPT13	18:27:43	450	440	462	439
BO N3	SOYBEAN OIL (OPEN OUTCRY)	SEPT13	18:29:06	46	45.31	48.35	44.27
ZL N3	SOYBEAN OIL	SEPT13	18:15:45	46	45.23	48.31	43.38
C N3	CORN (OPEN-OUTCRY)	SEPT13	18:30:33	650	651	655	647
ZC N3	CORN	SEPT13	18:38:01	650	650	654	646
O N3	OATS (OPEN OUTCRY)	SEPT13	18:45:54	409	406	412	401
ZO N3	OATS	SEPT13	18:25:34	409	408	410	403
W N3	WHEAT (OPEN OUTCRY)	SEPT13	18:30:01	687	693	695	687
ZW N3	WHEAT	SEPT13	18:48:59	687	690	697	685
RR N3	ROUGH RICE (OPEN OUTCRY)	SEPT13	18:18:28	1625	1621	1627	1615
KW N3	WHEAT (OPEN OUTCRY)	SEPT13	18:34:43	721	720	727	712

A party that agrees to buy an asset at some point in the future holds a long position in a futures contract, and the party that agrees to sell an asset at some point in the future holds a short position. As discussed in previous chapters, the item the seller has agreed to sell should be treated as a paper asset. A promise to sell something is only a promise, and until someone delivers that physical asset to the buyer, it should be treated as a paper asset. How can you prove that you physically own a particular asset? Physical ownership is represented by possession of a stock certificate, a deed of purchase, an option certificate, or even a register receipt. Thus, a futures contract remains a promise and its underlying paper assets shouldn't be counted toward or against a physical asset inventory (the asset portfolio).

Another important detail to keep in mind is that a futures contract's delivery is a very rare event—so rare that many industry professionals have little or no experience in handling the deliveries. To avoid making (or accepting) a delivery, an investor must close out his or her position, resulting in his or her entering into a contract on the same asset type with an opposite position compared to that of the original contract (that is, the buyer becomes a seller).

■ **Example**   An investor in Seattle decides that the price of crude oil will rise over the next six months. On April 15, 2014, this investor enters into a crude oil futures contract with the delivery date set for September 15, 2014. (The investor is holding a long position in this contract.) To avoid accepting a crude oil delivery, the investor will need to sell (or take a short position in) his current contract sometime in June to close out his futures position. The investor who sold the original September 15, 2014, futures contract can close out his short position by buying (or taking a long position in) the September 15, 2014, futures crude oil contract in either July or August 2014. The investor's total gain or loss will be determined by the difference in crude oil price between April 15, 2014, and the time at which the futures contract is closed out.

The *first notice day* signifies the first day an investor may submit a *notice of intent* to an exchange. Once a notice of intent is submitted, delivery can take place. This means that the two parties will need to prepare themselves for the delivery. The *last notice day* is the last day when such a notice of intent may be submitted to an exchange. Even the delivery of a futures contract could result in a cash settlement. For example, a futures contract on the S&P 500 typically will result in a cash settlement (otherwise one of the contract participants will have to physically deliver stock certificates, which is impractical and unrealistic).

Because futures contracts are regulated by official stock exchanges, great care is taken to unambiguously specify a valid list of *commodity grades* that will satisfy any given futures contract. Typically, financial assets are well defined and unambiguous. Commodities, on the other hand, have to be defined in detail, owing to significant variation of quality and appearance within the commodity class. If the delivered asset's grade falls outside of the exchange-specified grade range, then a specific discount must be applied. The following example illustrates the application of the concept to a futures contract, analogously to the example of the corn forward contract in Chapter 4.

■ **Example**   Deliverable grades of wheat shall contain a minimum of a 15 percent protein level. However, protein levels of less than 15 percent, but equal to or greater than 12.6 percent, are deliverable at a five-cent (5¢) discount to the contract price. Protein levels of less than 12.6 percent are not deliverable. As an investor, you expect to receive wheat of a certain quality. That quality may be described by a number of parameters, and the protein content is only one of them. If the protein content of the delivered goods is below the expected level, the investor will experience a loss when he or she attempts to resell the wheat. The exchange prevents this type of issue from happening by clearly and unambiguously specifying the quality of the expected assets and indicating what will happen if the asset quality falls outside of the exchange-specified range. In the example, a protein level of less than 12.6 percent is not acceptable and will be rejected by the investor and the exchange. The wheat with a protein level between 15 percent and 12.6 percent will be discounted from the agreed-on futures price.

Another essential feature of futures contracts is the *daily settlement procedure*. Consider an investor who wants to purchase two futures copper contracts. Each contract is for the purchase of 150 ounces of copper, so the investor purchases two contracts to obtain 300 ounces of copper. The current futures price of copper is US$100 per ounce. On September 1, 2014, the price of copper declines from $100 to $98.11. A decline in price means that the investor who is contracted to buy the copper at $100 per ounce is losing money. The investor's first day loss is:

$$300 * (-1.89) = \$567$$

To ensure that this investor will not default, the exchange will instruct him to maintain a *margin account*. Assume that the investor is directed to deposit $2,500 into his margin account per each contract (or $5,000 for the two contracts). Because the price of copper went down on September 1, the investor's margin account goes down by (see Table 5-2):

$$\$5,000 - \$567 = \$4,433$$

Table 5-2. Margin Account in Action

Day	Future Price ($)	Daily Gain ($)	Cumulative Gain ($)	Margin Account Balance ($)	Margin Call ($)
	$100.00			$5,000	
Sep. 1	$98.11	-$567	-$567	$4,433	
Sep. 2	$97.30	-$243	-$810	$4,190	
Sep. 3	$98.12	$246	$3	$4,436	
Sep. 4	$95.40	-$816	-$570	$3,620	
Sep. 5	$92.32	-$924	-$1,740	$2,696	$2,304
Sep. 6	$100.05	$2,319	$1,395	$5,015	
Sep. 7	$101.12	$321	$2,640	$5,336	
Sep. 8	$102.01	$267	$588	$5,603	
Sep. 9	$103.66	$495	$762	$6,098	
Sep. 10	$101.50	-$648	-$153	$5,450	
Sep. 11	$100.55	-$285	-$933	$5,165	
Sep. 12	$100.34	-$63	-$348	$5,102	
Sep. 13	$99.99	-$105	-$168	$4,997	
Sep. 14	$99.98	-$3	-$108	$4,994	
Sep. 15	$100.06	$24	$21	$5,018	

The exchange also determines the additional margin, called a *maintenance margin*, which acts as a trigger indicating that the investor should put more money into his margin account, up to the *initial margin*.

Because the contract requirements dictate and constrain the ultimate design (and not the other way around), they are the business rules that will shape and mold the starter data models. (Bear in mind that, as usual in this book, the models are broken into multiple subject areas to keep the diagrams more focused and concise). The basic requirements of a futures contract are the following:

- Futures contracts involve at least two parties:

  - A party that wants to purchase or sell an asset at some point in the future. (The asset specified in the futures contract is a paper asset.)

  - A broker working for an exchange, holding an opposite position (long or short). (Once again, these assets should be treated as paper assets.)

- Each contract may be closed out prior to its expiration date, leading to another futures contract with an opposite position compared to the original contract.

- Futures contracts may result in physical delivery.

- Each party engaged in a futures contract is usually asked to maintain an exchange-controlled margin account.

- Great care is usually taken to unambiguously specify a valid range of commodity grades that will satisfy a particular consumption asset in the scope of a given futures contract. The modeler's job is to store and maintain this range and associate it with a proper variable.

This list of futures contract requirements bears a resemblance to those of other financial contracts—especially forward contracts. Granted, the mechanics that govern the inner workings of futures contracts are more complex than those of other contract types owing to the imposition of exchange regulations. But breaking down the exchange-imposed business rules into smaller and more manageable steps facilitates the task of applying the principles you've already learned and shaping them to meet your current business needs.

Modeling Employment

Let's begin our futures contract modeling exercise with a simple task: modeling the employment relationship. You may be wondering why we discuss employment within the context of futures contracts. The answer is simple: futures contracts are exchange-driven and always involve a broker on one side of the contract.

In general, employment is modeled as a relationship between two parties: a PERSON and an ORGANIZATION (Figure 5-1). Can one person employ another person, or can organization employ another organization? It all depends on the underlying business requirements. You may have to account for the fact that a person may employ another person. In such cases, draw two generic relationships between the PARTY and EMPLOYMENT entities.

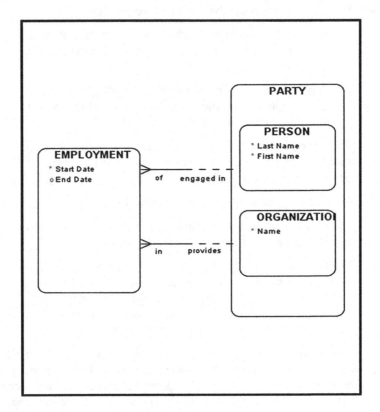

Figure 5-1. Modeling an employment relationship

An interesting feature of the EMPLOYMENT entity (a relationship that is modeled as an entity) is that it looks similar to the CONTRACT. In fact, EMPLOYMENT may be viewed as a type of contract between a PERSON and an ORGANIZATION, for which the start date attribute signifies the beginning of the employment and the end date attribute signifies the ending of it. Incidentally, the marriage relationship is modeled similarly, involving a relationship between one PERSON and another PERSON.

Subtyping Futures Contracts

Let's proceed to another simple exercise: subtyping the CONTRACT TYPE (a supertype) into the following two subtypes (Figure 5-2):

- FUTURES CONTRACT TYPE
- OTHER TYPE.

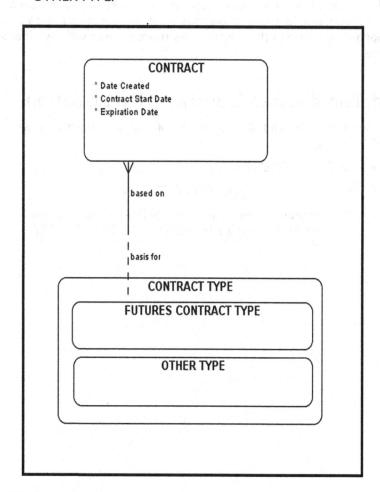

Figure 5-2. Futures contract subtype

This subtyping allows us to neatly specify the type of contract we are modeling to avoid any ambiguities and conflicts later in the context of a larger data model. Keep in mind that each contract type supports a specific set of business requirements and rules. By explicitly associating a specific CONTRACT TYPE with a CONTRACT, we implicitly specify the underlying business rules and end user understanding. Business professionals working in the financial sector will understand these business rules as long as they can clearly and unambiguously identify a given contract type.

Simplicity and clarity should be your top priority when creating conceptual data models. The end goal for your modeling exercises is to be understood and gain support among your peers and various user groups. Paying close attention to details such as proper subtype use will keep your model presentations concise, simple, and unambiguous. I highly recommend that you follow this approach because in the long run this thoroughness will pay off and save you time.

Modeling Futures Contracts Participation

Figure 5-3 assembles and displays some of the building blocks we've just learned, including:

- An EMPLOYMENT entity

- A properly subtyped CONTRACT TYPE

- The relationship between the CONTRACT and a proper contract type (namely, a FUTURES CONTRACT TYPE)

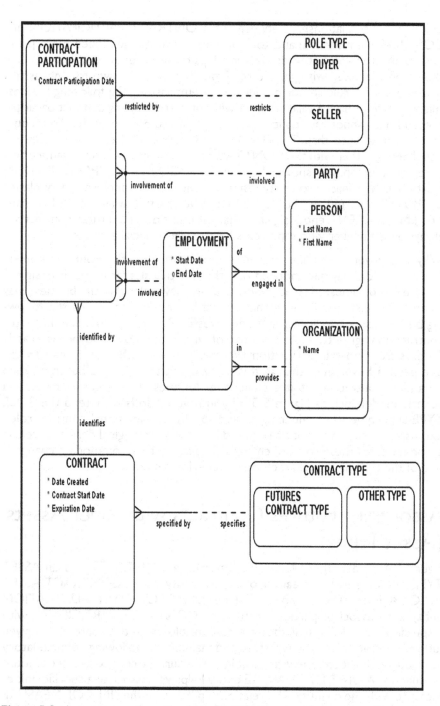

Figure 5-3. Associating parties with a futures contract

Note that the relationship between the CONTRACT PARTICIPATION and CONTRACT entities is mandatory on both sides. As mentioned twice previously, mandatory-on-both-sides relationships occur infrequently in practice and should be examined with great care. Typically, they are drawn to emphasize a specific business rule. In our model we are emphasizing the following business rule: one cannot have a valid contract without corresponding contract participation, and one cannot have contract participation without a contract. To account for this, make sure that CONTRACT PARTICIPATION entity instances are populated together with the CONTRACT and packaged within the same transaction. In addition, you should document that CONTRACT PARTICIPATION must contain at least two entity instances: one for the employee/party playing the BUYER role, and another for the employee/party playing the SELLER role. The EMPLOYMENT entity signifies that on one side of a futures contract we always have a broker who represents a particular financial exchange.

Why are buyer and seller attributes not stored on the contract level in Figure 5-3? You may have noticed that the way this starter model is designed, it can easily be adjusted to accommodate any new roles that the business may identify. For instance, imagine that you've been asked to model the following business scenario: investor A and investor B have signed a simple barter contract and agree to exchange a ton of wheat for a ton of soybeans exactly 60 days from now. In a situation like this, you will either be forced to call one party a buyer even though this party is not technically a buyer, or keep on adding contract attributes to account for these new contract roles. In a generic model such as Figure 5-3, all you have to do is to extend the ROLE TYPE supertype (thus widening it) and specify any additional contract roles. Extensive redesign will not be required because your original design gracefully accommodates these types of changes. The ability to accommodate change is one of the criteria that characterize a superior data model.

Associating Futures Contracts with Paper Assets (Asset Types)

Figure 5-4 models the relationship between a CONTRACT and an ASSET TYPE, resulting in the creation of a new entity called CONTRACT ASSET ALLOCATION. The purpose of the CONTRACT ASSET ALLOCATION entity is to associate parties through the CONTRACT PARTICIPANT with a specific ASSET TYPE that they are responsible for in the context of a given futures contract. Here you will store and maintain the following nonmandatory attributes (whichever one is applicable in the current context), either amount or quantity. A UNIT OF MEASURE entity helps you associate a specific unit of measure with the quantity. The relationship between the UNIT OF MEASURE and the CONTRACT ASSET ALLOCATION is nonmandatory on both sides. This is by design because the unit of measure specification (in the context of the CONTRACT ASSET ALLOCATION) depends on the nature of the ASSET TYPE and may be entirely optional. You saw a similar model in the context of forward contracts and are familiar with most of its features by now.

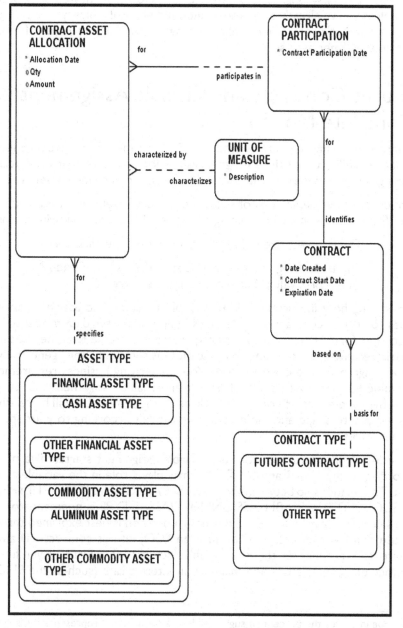

Figure 5-4. Associating futures contracts with paper assets (asset types)

I emphasize again that, on the CONTRACT ASSET ALLOCATION level, futures contracts should be related to ASSET TYPES and not physical ASSETS. Relating futures contracts to physical assets would mean that the underlying assets in question could be counted toward or against an investor's asset portfolio. This is wrong, as futures contracts should be viewed as promises and, unless you've already accepted an inbound physical delivery or a cash settlement, I strongly recommend that you treat the underlying assets of futures contracts as paper assets.

Futures Contracts and Variable Assignment (Complete Model)

An interesting challenge arises when we have to model and account for an exchange's ability to specify a range of values for a variable that is associated with a given asset type—in the present instance, a commodity asset type.

Consider, for example, an investor who enters into a frozen concentrated orange juice (FCOJ) futures contract holding a long position on the following terms:

- The contract size is 15,000 pounds of orange juice solids.

- The underlying asset's grade is specified as "US Grade A with a Brix value[1] between 35 and 55 degrees."

Considering how important it is to be able to store and assign a range of values to certain contract variables, let's build the starter data model so that it accounts for this critical business requirement. Assume that the allocation of variables (including the range specification) is specified either generically by an exchange or at the contract level. Your underlying business requirements will guide you on how to model particular variable assignments. Once you know the general pattern of the variable assignment model, it will be relatively easy for you to shape and mold your own models according to your specific business rules.

Figure 5-5 depicts a futures contract variable assignment starter data model. According to the model, an ASSET TYPE may play a role in the variable assignment. The relationship between the VARIABLE ASSIGNMENT/ASSET TYPE and the SUGGESTED VARIABLE ASSIGNMENT/ASSET TYPE is nonmandatory on both sides. The reasoning behind this design decision is best explained through the use of a few examples. For instance, an FCOJ futures contract will always require us to account for the Brix variable. However, to valuate a given futures contract, one should store and maintain an interest rate (such as the LIBOR),

---

[1]*Brix value* identifies the percent of sugar solids in a product and represents the strength of the solution as percentage by weight.

which has no bearing on the underlying asset type. To generalize, an ASSET TYPE may play a role in the VARIABLE ASSIGNMENT/SUGGESTED VARIABLE ASSIGNMENT, but its presence is not required (depending on the context).

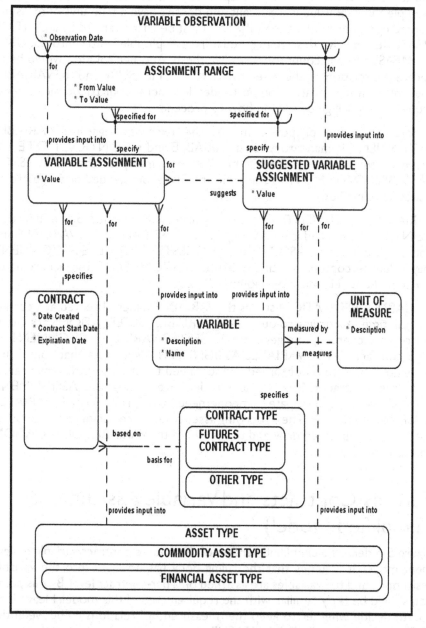

Figure 5-5. Futures contract variable assignment and range specification (complete model)

ASSIGNMENT RANGE allows us to attach a range of suitable values to a particular VARIABLE. For example, if the specified Brix value is between 35 and 55 degrees, we should first create a variable with the name set to Brix. Its range specification will be stored in the ASSIGNMENT RANGE with the *from* and *to* values set to 35 and 55, respectively. Incidentally, in our hypothetical example the Brix value is a percent and doesn't have a true unit of measure. According to our model, the VARIABLE must be characterized by a UNIT OF MEASURE. To solve this, we may add a "Not Applicable" entry into the UNIT OF MEASURE to account for cases like these. Another solution would be to update the relationship between the UNIT OF MEASURE and the VARIABLE and make it nonmandatory on both sides. In general, your particular business requirements will guide you on how to proceed.

According to the proposed model, the exchange-suggested VARIABLE ASSIGNMENT is mandatory for a VARIABLE and a CONTRACT TYPE and nonmandatory for an ASSET TYPE. You may interpret the SUGGESTED VARIABLE ASSIGNMENT as something that is recommended or suggested by a specific ruling body.

VARIABLE ASSIGNMENT, on the other hand, is performed on an individual CONTRACT level and is mandatory for a CONTRACT and a VARIABLE and nonmandatory for an ASSET TYPE. SUGGESTED VARIABLE ASSIGNMENT may influence contract-specific VARIABLE ASSIGNMENTS, but according to our model this relationship is nonmandatory.

VARIABLE OBSERVATION stores the VARIABLE values observed at a certain point in time. According to our model, VARIABLE OBSERVATIONS are either performed according to a generic SUGGESTED VARIABLE ASSIGNMENT or on a contract-specific VARIABLE ASSIGNMENT level. Note that some variables don't have to be observed and just need to be initialized. For instance, once the contract's Brix variable is initialized using the ASSIGNMENT RANGE, we don't anticipate someone needing to make periodic VARIABLE OBSERVATIONS of it. The underlying asset type's price volatility, on the other hand, may be observed daily, and this is where the VARIABLE OBSERVATION comes in handy.

Futures Contracts and Variable Assignment (Simplified Model)

Figure 5-6 depicts a simplified version of the futures contract variable assignment model. It assumes that the ruling body has no input into the variable assignment and the variables are assigned on a per-contract level. By this point, you should be fairly familiar with the requirements of this model. I leave it to you to decide whether to keep the "measured by" relationship between the VARIABLE and the UNIT OF MEASURE as mandatory. Remember that some variables simply do not have a true unit of measure. In such cases, either make the relationship nonmandatory or create a catchall "Not Available" entry in the UNIT OF MEASURE.

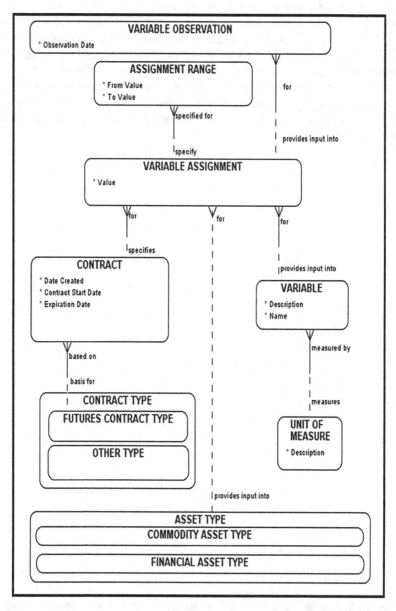

Figure 5-6. Futures contract variable assignment and range specifications (simplified model)

Futures Contracts and Variable Observations

Some of the variables associated with a given contract (either through the VARIABLE ASSIGNMENT or SUGGESTED VARIABLE ASSIGNMENT) are typically observed throughout the life of that contract. The resulting observations should be stored in an entity called VARIABLE OBSERVATION (Figure 5-7; see also Figures 5-5 and 5-6). Prudent investors often like to valuate their contracts daily. To do so, one needs daily to record variables such as the asset type's spot price and the interest rate (the LIBOR or the risk-free interest rate, for instance). Being able to observe and store market variables on a daily basis opens a number of possibilities, from computing asset price volatilities to extrapolating future interest rate movements based on existing historical data.[2]

---

[2]The models in Figures 5-5 through 5-7 are based on Hay's models demonstrating how variables can be initialized and observed within the context of "the laboratory," as presented in David C. Hay, *Data Model Patterns: Conventions of Thought*, Dorset House, 1995; and idem, *Data Model Patterns: A Metadata Map*, Morgan Kaufmann, 2006.

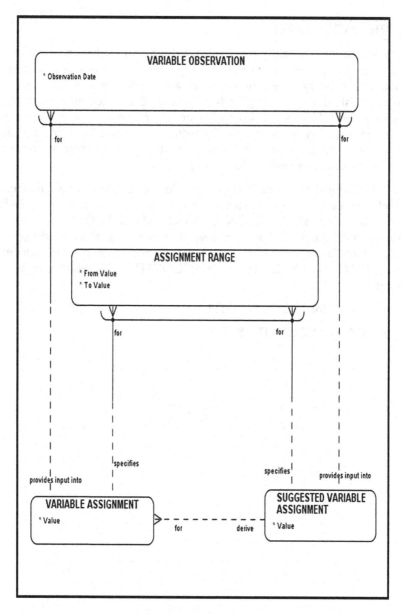

Figure 5-7. Futures contracts and variable observations

Margin Accounts

A margin account is a safety mechanism used by an exchange to make sure that a given party does not default. Margin accounts have built-in triggers that alert each party when funds are at a dangerously low level and have to be replenished. Once a trigger has been fired, an account owner has to act quickly and add more funds to his or her margin account. An inability to do so in a speedy manner typically results in various fines and penalties. The mechanics behind a given margin account are rather straightforward, as shown by the example given in Table 5-2).

Figure 5-8 diagrams a futures contract margin account. An ACCOUNT entity is modeled as a contract between an employee (of an exchange) and a PARTY (which may be either a PERSON or an ORGANIZATION). An exchange employee (a broker) works with investors, assisting them with opening new accounts. An account has "date created" and "date closed" attributes. An ACCOUNT must be based on an ACCOUNT TYPE, which can be sub-typed into:

- MARGIN ACCOUNT TYPE
- CASH ACCOUNT TYPE.

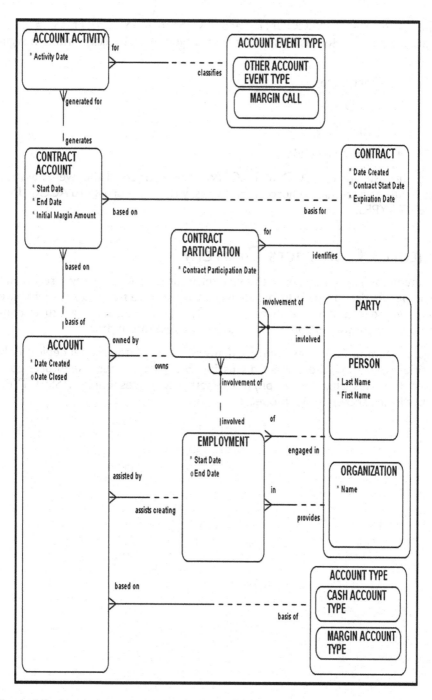

Figure 5-8. Futures contract margin account model

The CONTRACT ACCOUNT becomes the margin account for a given futures contract. Here is a list of attributes typically associated with a margin account:

1. Start Date

2. End Date

3. Initial Margin

4. Maintenance Margin

The purpose of the ACCOUNT ACTIVITY is to trace all the events associated with a given margin account and classify them according to ACCOUNT EVENT TYPES.

Futures Contracts Delivery

As mentioned at the outset of this chapter, futures contracts very rarely result in actual physical delivery. In fact, deliveries are so rare that most traders have only a vague idea of how to handle them. Typically, a position in a futures contract is closed out well before that contract's expiration date.

Figure 5-9 models futures contract delivery. As usual, the model depicts only entities relevant to the current discussion. For instance, because futures contract deliveries only involve physical assets, any corresponding ASSET TYPE entity is not shown in the model.

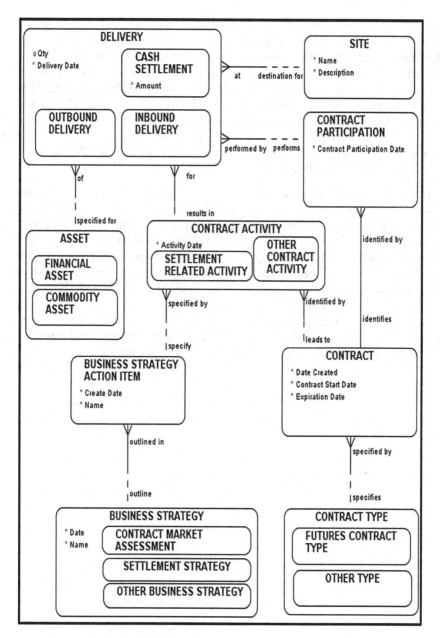

Figure 5-9. Model of futures contract delivery

Typically, an organization will identify and specify critical business strategies well in advance. In this section, we discuss delivery subject area and, thus, we'll call the BUSINESS STRATEGY we're working with the SETTLEMENT STRATEGY. The BUSINESS STRATEGY ACTION ITEM entity associates potentially multiple activities with a given BUSINESS STRATEGY; the CONTRACT ACTIVITY entity, in turn, associates these BUSINESS STRATEGY ACTION ITEMS with a given CONTRACT. For example, the intent to deliver activity is an example of a BUSINESS STRATEGY ACTION ITEM; if this activity is executed on behalf of a given contract, it will be stored in the CONTRACT ACTIVITY, grouped under the SETTLEMENT RELATED ACTIVITY.

If physical delivery does happen, we have to make sure that the delivered physical asset satisfies the contract-specific quality criteria. This is where our initialized and observed variables (along with our assignment range) come in handy. Figure 5-10 depicts a model that relates "marked for delivery" physical assets with variables, storing the resulting assignment in the DELIVERY VARIABLE ASSIGNMENT entity. Once the assignment is complete, these variables can be observed and stored in the VARIABLE OBSERVATION entity. These VARIABLE OBSERVATIONS should be checked against the exchange-approved ASSIGNMENT RANGE to make sure they satisfy the necessary quality criteria. The actual process of data validation cannot be shown in our model and will be designed separately by process architects.

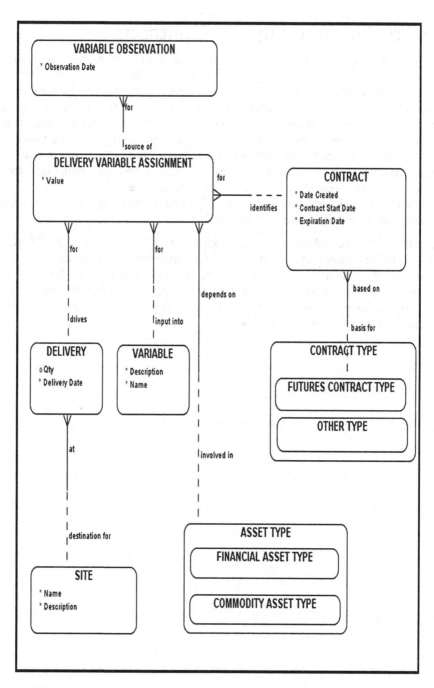

Figure 5-10. Futures contract and delivery variable assignment model

Rolling Forward Futures Contracts

Sometimes a hedge is needed on a date that is further in the future than the delivery date of any of the tradable contracts. For instance, an investor might like to lock in the price of a certain amount of copper 10 years from now. Imagine that the maximum delivery date of any of the publicly tradable contracts goes forward up to six years. In a case like this, the investor may roll the hedge forward by closing one contract and taking the same position in another futures contract with a later delivery date. This process may be repeated numerous times until the desired future date is reached. Note that under a perfectly executed *rolling forward* scheme, there should be no time gap (or time slippage), between a closing order and an opening order. Slippages cause a loss of profit and should be avoided.

A rolling forward scheme can be implemented by using a CONTRACT STRUCTURE entity (Figure 5-11). The challenge here is to track all of the contracts that participated in the rolling forward scheme and be able to unravel an entire scheme from the first contract (and all the way up to the last). Rolling forward is just one of the many trading strategy schemes that you should be able to store and classify.

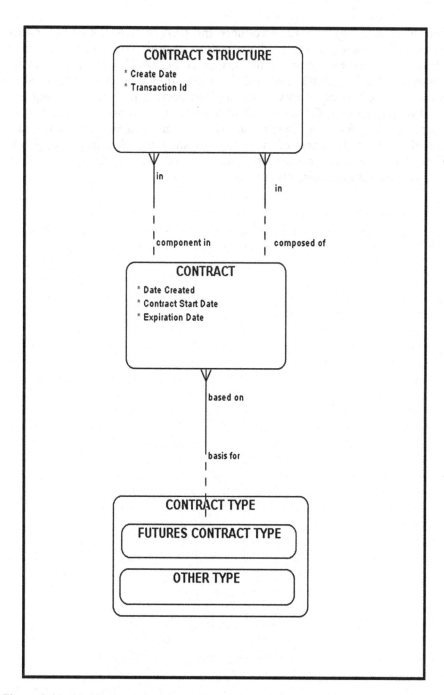

Figure 5-11. Model of a rolling forward futures contract

The diagram in Figure 5-12 introduces the CLASSIFICATION TYPE entity, which we discussed briefly in the previous chapter. The classification type allows us to easily group and classify related CONTRACT STRUCTURE entity instances. The ROLLING FORWARD classification subtype may be used to unravel entire sets of futures contracts that became part of the rolling forward trading scheme. Of course, all of the futures contracts that are part of the same rolling forward scheme will share the same trading scheme transaction identifier so that users of the model will know that they belong together. These are, of course, implementation details, which typically are dependent on your unique business rules and needs.

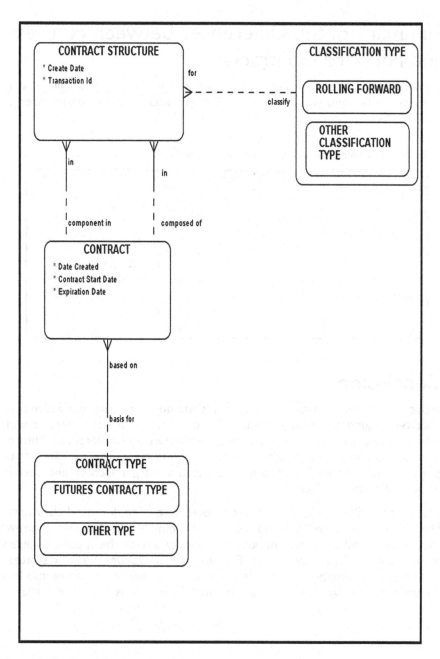

Figure 5-12. Classifying contract structure

Summary of the Differences between Futures and Forward Contracts

Forward and futures contracts are two important hedging strategies that in many respects contrast with and complement each other, as summarized in the Table 5-3.

Table 5-3. Contrasting futures and forward contracts

Forward Contracts	Futures Contract
Not regulated	Regulated by an exchange
Non-standardized	Standardized
Have one (and only one) specific delivery date	Have a range of delivery dates
Very risky	An exchange minimizes their risk of default; hence, they are considered less risky
Result either in cash settlement, delivery, or default	Typically are closed out prior to the contract reaching maturity
Settled on the last day of the contract	Settled daily by using a margin account

Conclusion

In this chapter we discussed the important and hugely popular derivative contract type called a futures contract. We contrasted futures contracts with forward contracts and identified their similarities and differences. Futures contracts are exchange-regulated and hence less risky. The exchange mitigates the risk of default with a feature called a margin account and certain associated built-in triggers.

The basic building blocks used in this chapter have been discussed elsewhere. This chapter assembled the data modeling building blocks discussed in previous chapters and shaped or molded them according to the specific business requirements of futures contracts. The next chapter applies the same strategy to options. By helping your models manage complexity and accommodate variation and change, modeling patterns make your life as a modeler easier.

Modeling Options

We have now indicated the two operations of our understanding, intuition and deduction, on which alone we have said we must rely in the acquisition of knowledge.

—René Descartes, *Regulae ad Directionem Ingenii*

Previous chapters familiarized you with futures and forward contracts, which allow investors to lock in future asset prices either in the OTC market (as in forward contracts) or in an exchange-controlled environment (as in futures contracts). You learned how their respective business requirements should be modeled and how to design data structures to accommodate their respective business rules. This chapter follows the same overall pattern in modeling another important derivative instrument: the option.

An *option*, in lay terms, is a type of insurance that gives an investor a right but not an obligation to buy or sell the underlying paper asset. If market conditions become unfavorable, the investor who purchases an option can safely walk away from the deal. Options are traded on financial exchanges and in the OTC markets. For example, the CBOE is the largest options exchange in the world.

There are two types of option contracts (Figure 6-1):

- A *call* option allows an investor to buy the underlying asset for a certain price.

- A *put* option allows an investor to sell the underlying asset for a certain price.

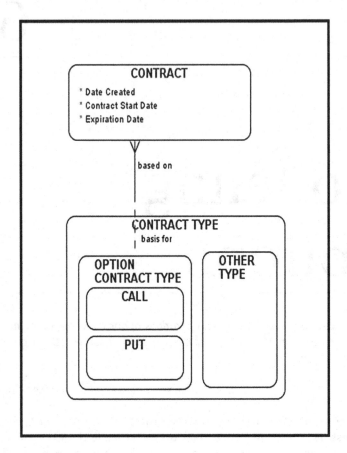

Figure 6-1. Modeling option types

All the call options or all the put options of a particular underlying asset are said to belong to the same *option class*. For instance, Oracle Corporation (ORCL) call options belong to one option class and ORCL put options belong to another option class.

The underlying asset price in a given option contract is called the *strike price* and indicates the price at which an investor can purchase the underlying asset (such as a stock) on a particular date. The date when the option contract expires is called the *expiration date*, meaning that after this date the option contract becomes worthless and ceases to exist.

On an exchange, options are packaged and sold in units called *contracts* (aka *standardized contracts*). Each standardized stock option contract typically contains 100 shares. For example, an investor who purchases 10 standardized Apple call option contracts has acquired a right (again, not an obligation) to purchase 1,000 Apple shares at some point in the future at a preset strike price. Of course, the investor in question may choose not to exercise his or her purchasing right if market conditions become unfavorable.

At what point should an investor exercise the right to purchase the underlying asset? It all depends on the *option style* type (Figure 6-2). One option style is called the *European*. This particular style can only be exercised upon the option expiration date. Alternatively, *American options* can be exercised at any time prior to the expiration date. An American option style is the most popular because it provides the most flexibility. *Bermudan options* may be exercised on a preapproved range of dates. (The geographic names of the option styles are arbitrary, except that "Bermudan" is a play on blending American and European.)

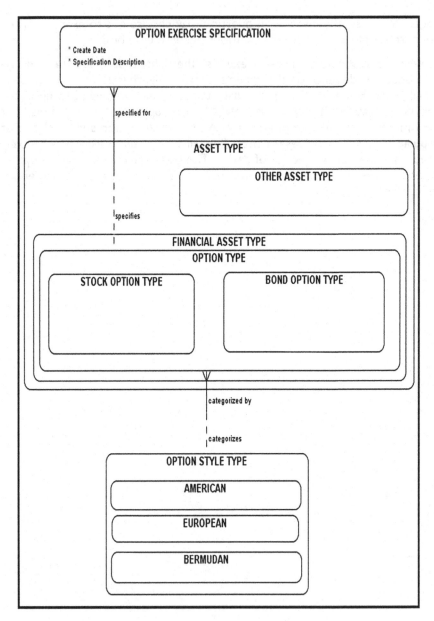

Figure 6-2. Modeling options and option style types

Note that the OPTION STYLE TYPE is related to the OPTION TYPE (a paper asset). The OPTION EXERCISE SPECIFICATION stores detailed specifications regarding when the option in question may be exercised. For example, a Bermudan option exercise specification might say that the buyer may exercise the option only on the first or the fifteenth days of each month.

Options provide investors with the ability to purchase something. However, investors don't have to exercise their right to buy this something. The option's owner may safely walk away from the deal if the market conditions become unfavorable. The downside is that an investor has to purchase an option contract beforehand. Here you should be able to spot the difference between futures or forward contracts and option contracts: it costs nothing to get into futures or forward contracts. Option contracts, on the other hand, cost money from the start.

An option contract's underlying assets are paper assets. An option is directly linked with (or points to) a specific asset type (for simplicity's sake we discuss stock option contracts here and assume that the underlying asset is a specific stock). This asset type is classified as a paper asset and shouldn't be counted toward or against a physical asset inventory. Transformation of these underlying asset types into actual, physical assets occurs when the options get exercised and physical assets are exchanged. (An option's delivery mechanism is examined in the "Modeling an Option's Delivery Subject Area" section.)

A simple example serves to illustrate how option contracts work.

Example   Assume that today is December 1, 2014. An investor is interested in purchasing Apple Corporation shares and is convinced that the price of these shares will dramatically increase by June 2015. The investor purchases one European-style option contract for $150 (the cost of the option), which allows him to purchase 100 Apple Corporation shares for US$200 (per share). Please note that $150 is the option price and has to be paid up front. The option contract expires on June 1, 2015. The investor who has purchased this option is taking a long position. On the opposite end of this contract is an investor who has agreed to sell 100 Apple shares on June 1, 2015, for $200 per share. The investor who sold this option took a short position.

Assume that on June 1, 2015, the Apple shares go up in price with each share costing $220 on the spot market. The first investor decides to exercise his right to purchase the Apple shares and buys 100 Apple shares for $200 (per share) when the market price (or the spot price) of each share is $220. The first investor (with a long position in this option contract) has just made a profit of [($220 − $200) * 100] − $150 = $1,850. Note that we subtract $150 from our profit calculations because this is what investor A paid up front to obtain the option.

Consider the alternative scenario of an inverse variation on the second paragraph of preceding example.

■ **Same Example with Variation**   Suppose the price of the Apple stock plunges to $180 on June 1, 2015. In this case the investor has the right to purchase 100 Apple shares for $200, even though their market spot price is just $180 per share. The option gives the investor the ability to simply walk away from the deal, thus costing him only the original $150 he spent on the option.

Option Positions

There are four types of option positions:

- Call buyer (requires a long position in a call option)
- Put buyer (requires a long position in a put option)
- Call seller (requires a short position in a call option)
- Put seller (requires a short position in a put option)

Option buyers hold *long positions*. Option sellers hold *short positions*. Selling an option is sometimes called *writing an option*.

Offsetting Orders

Offsetting is a method that reverses the original transaction and exits the trade. A few simple scenarios illustrate how to properly offset a given order. A party that has bought an option may close the position by issuing an offsetting order to sell the same option, with the same strike price and expiration date. The opposite is also true; a party may write an option and, later on, close out that position by entering into an offsetting order to buy the same option with the same strike price and expiration date. If any of these steps are not specifically followed, the original position stays active.

For example, assume that an investor purchases a call option and later sells a call option on the same underlying asset, but with a different strike price. The investor may have reduced his risk, but he didn't close his position and instead has two active positions. Why? Because the strike price in the above-mentioned transactions is different.

Underlying Assets

Option contracts may be linked to numerous assets. The following is a short list of asset types that an option may be linked to (or point to):

- Stocks

- Currencies

- Futures

- Stock indices

This chapter discusses and models options on stocks. Modeling other underlying asset types is generally done in a similar fashion, so the skills you learn here will easily translate to them. Stock options are predominantly traded on financial exchanges such as the Philadelphia Stock Exchange (PHLX, www. phlx.com) and the American Stock Exchange (AMEX, www.amex.com). Recall that one standardized option contract typically involves purchasing 100 shares of stock. Options may be purchased on a wide variety of stocks.

The option price is directly dependent on the following:

- The option contract's expiration date (treated as the contract's attribute),

- The strike price (treated as the contract's attribute),

- The underlying asset price (directly observable in the market),

- The time to expiration (derivable data),

- The asset price volatility (indirectly calculated and maintained via market variables),

- Any dividends paid out on the stock during the life of the option (directly observable in the market)

- The LIBOR rate or any other rate that an organization is interested in keeping track of (directly observable in the market).

Of these, the stock's implied volatility is calculated (and recalculated) daily based on the historical stock price data. These calculations involve a heavy use of statistical models and are resource-intensive. However, because volatility plays such an important role in deriving an option's price, financial organizations are very interested in knowing what it is. I perform a sample derivation of the ORCL stock price volatility in the "Calculating Volatility from Historical Data" section to show the underlying analytical technique and the challenges (related to performance and storage) that large financial institutions typically face when performing these types of calculations on a large scale. In general, volatility is just one element of a complicated option pricing mechanism that has many moving parts. Most financial shops develop their own sophisticated mathematical models that try to approximate option prices and predict the future direction these prices may take.

Associating Option Contracts with Buyers and Sellers

Figure 6-3 diagrams the various relationships between a given contract and the involved parties (as well as the roles these parties play in a given contract).

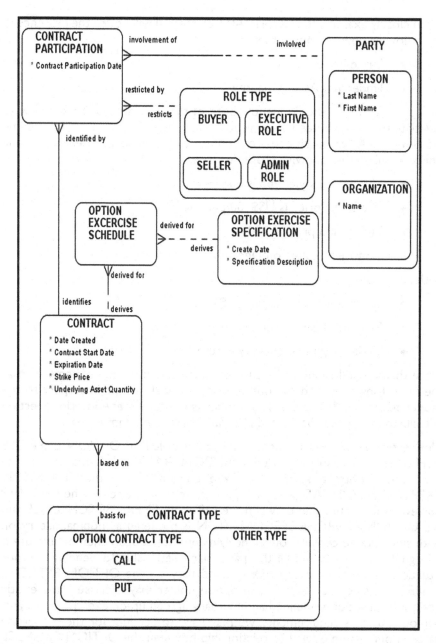

Figure 6-3. Associating option contracts with buyers and sellers

If you closely examine the CONTRACT entity, you will notice the presence of the following new attributes, the:

- Strike Price
- Underlying Asset Quantity

An option contract should identify both of these attributes. To see how to populate these attributes, let's look at a simple hypothetical example. Assume that investor A has purchased a call option to purchase 10 Intel shares. The option exhibits the following characteristics:

- The option style type is European.
- The strike price is US$100 per share.
- The option price is $50.
- Contract expires on December 1, 2014.

In this example:

- Strike price is initialized to $100.
- Expiration date is set to December 1, 2014.
- Underlying asset quantity is set to 10.

Note that we still cannot fully describe this particular option; items such as the underlying asset and the option price are still missing in respect to the model depicted in Figure 6-3. The "Modeling Option Asset Allocation" section will illustrate how to specify and populate these important items.

Notice that Figure 6-3 introduces an entity called an OPTION EXERCISE SCHEDULE. This entity is related to the CONTRACT and identifies a set of all the possible contract exercise dates. We've taken the view that the OPTION EXERCISE SPECIFICATION may affect the option exercise schedule's data; however, the relationship between the OPTION EXERCISE SCHEDULE and the OPTION EXERCISE SPECIFICATION is modeled as nonmandatory on both sides. Please consult your underlying business documentation and use it as a guide on how to model this particular relationship (depending on your situation, you may have to make it mandatory on the OPTION EXERCISE SCHEDULE side). For instance, an option holder may exercise some exotic options on a set of predefined and mutually agreed up-on exercise dates and, per our business requirements, we may have to account for these exercise dates in our data model. The relationship between the OPTION EXERCISE SCHEDULE and the CONTRACT is nonmandatory on the CONTRACT side because some options may explicitly specify only one exercise date, which we can then logically equate to the contract's expiration date (as is the case with European options, for instance). From there, we can generalize that in some cases a given option's exercise date is to be derived from a given contract's expiration date. However, one might argue that treating the exercise date as an expiration date is misleading and could potentially introduce various ambiguities and misunderstandings. After all, the underlying definition (typically found in the mapping documentation) of the contract's potential exercise date is different from the definition of the contract's expiration date. In this particular case, deriving one date from another blurs the distinction between these concepts and could cause various data anomalies. To play devil's advocate, I say that typically, deriving one attribute from another is a common practice if (and this is a very big *if*) the proposed design is supplemented by clear and concise documentation.

In this chapter we are modeling OTC option contracts—hence the absence of the EMPLOYMENT and MARGIN ACCOUNT entities. I do this to simplify the diagrams and steer you clear of misunderstandings or ambiguities. All of the building blocks necessary to model exchange-controlled option contracts were discussed in the preceding chapter. With a little practice, you should be able to incorporate them into your final designs with relative ease.

The CONTRACT PARTICIPATION entity keeps track of all of the parties that participate in a given option contract, along with the corresponding ROLES they might play. Note the presence of the mandatory relationship between the CONTRACT PARTICIPATION and CONTRACT entities. A valid option contract must involve at least two participants: the party that has purchased an option contract (the party holding a long position) and the party that has sold an option contract (the party holding a short position). We may also treat an option as insurance and say that a given option contract will always have an investor who has purchased insurance and an investor who has sold this insurance.

As discussed in previous chapters, the mandatory relationship between the CONTRACT PARTICIPATION entity and the CONTRACT entity implies that these entities have to be populated within the same transaction.

With the current design, you can easily describe and eventually reconstruct any type of option position (put buyer, call seller, and so forth) and the associated exercise dates.

Modeling an Option Asset Type

This and the following sections examine the internal anatomy of an option, peeling away layers of functionality to expose the inner workings of its intricate mechanism.

To repeat, it is advisable to treat an option's underlying asset as an asset type (paper asset). By itself, a stock option is insurance that is associated with (or points to) a specific asset type. The link between the option and the option's underlying specific asset type is always present. When purchased, options provide investors with the ability to buy a specific physical asset (Intel stock, for instance) at a future date. Unless the option is exercised, it should always point to a specific ASSET TYPE. Upon exercise, a physical ASSET is received and that asset should be counted toward or against the overall portfolio. If an option is left unexercised it expires, worthless. Once purchased, a stock option by itself is an asset and should be accounted for in your organization's accounting books. Moreover, options are subjected to stringent tax regulations and should be tracked very carefully.

Figure 6-4 models the STOCK OPTION ASSET TYPE as a paper asset. Do you remember how to differentiate between an asset and an asset type? An asset is something that you own, something you can hold in your hand: an option certificate, a register receipt, a platinum bar, a wad of cash, a stock certificate, and so on. An asset type, on the other hand, is a blueprint for a thing—something that you don't own and cannot hold or show to prove that it is yours. The opportunity to purchase a stock option may be modeled as illustrated in Figure 6-4, a STOCK OPTION ASSET TYPE (a subtype of the FINANCIAL ASSET TYPE) that points to a specific STOCK TYPE (another subtype of the FINANCIAL ASSET TYPE).

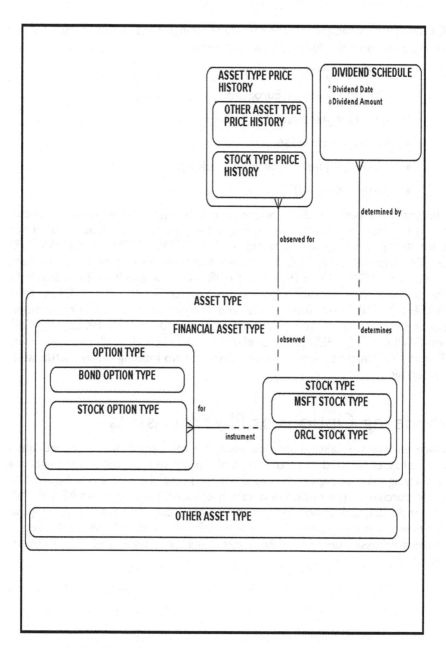

Figure 6-4. Model of an option asset type

A hypothetical example should help clarify things. Let's say an investor writes a call option with the following characteristics:

- Underlying asset quantity: one.

- Option style type: European.

- Contract start date: July 1, 2014.

- Option price: US$6.

- Underlying asset type: Intel stock type.

- Strike price: $20.

This yet-to-be-purchased call option that the investor hopes to sell is treated as a paper asset and is modeled in Figure 6-4. The resulting Intel stock option price depends on numerous things, such as STOCK TYPE PRICE HISTORY and DIVIDEND SCHEDULE. To account for these dependencies, we explicitly model the STOCK TYPE PRICE HISTORY and the DIVIDEND SCHEDULE entities and their relationships to the STOCK TYPE. The STOCK TYPE PRICE HISTORY contains not just the current open and closing numbers but also the historical data. In this model, the STOCK TYPE PRICE HISTORY and DIVIDEND SCHEDULE are related to the STOCK TYPE (a paper asset). This makes sense because the stock price has no bearing on the actual asset ownership.

Modeling Options as Physical Assets

Once an investor takes a long position in a call option, he or she obtains a physical asset (an option certificate) and a promise from the seller to sell the underlying asset (a paper asset at this point) (see the diagram in Figure 6-5). Once purchased, the option in question is transformed from an ASSET TYPE into an ASSET, and its new owner obtains an option certificate (meaning that the new option may be sold together with other valuable physical assets; it remains an asset until it either is exercised or expires and thus becomes worthless).

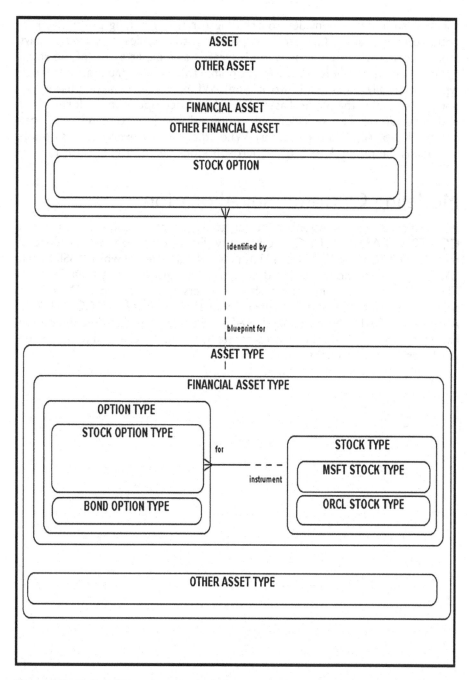

Figure 6-5. Model of an option as a physical asset

Suppose an investor considers purchasing (or taking a long position in) an option on one share of Microsoft Corporation stock. Unless this investor pays money for it, the option in question is treated as a paper asset (of the stock option asset type) that is related to (or points to) another paper asset: a stock type (specifically, a Microsoft stock type). When the investor purchases this option, he obtains the physical asset, the actual stock option in the form of the option certificate. This specific stock option will continue to point to the specific stock type (again, a paper asset). When the investor exercises this option, he obtains the physical asset (the Microsoft stock certificate) in return.

Modeling Option Asset Allocation

At the heart of the option's contract asset allocation subject area is the CONTRACT ASSET ALLOCATION entity (Figure 6-6). The main purpose of the CONTRACT ASSET ALLOCATION is to keep track of which ASSET each PARTY is responsible for within the context of a given option CONTRACT. This model maintains and stores physical assets, not asset types. Once both parties enter into an option contract, you should relate the CONTRACT ASSET ALLOCATION to the physical ASSETS because by that time the option has been purchased and the physical assets have been exchanged (cash for the stock certificate, for example).

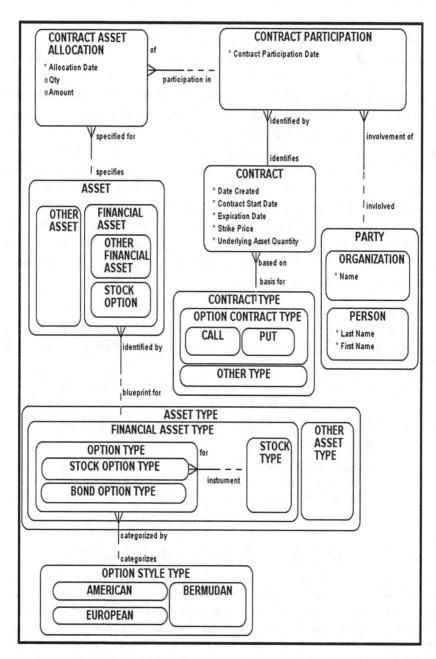

Figure 6-6. Modeling option asset allocations

■ **Example**   Assume that today is June 1, 2014. Investor B writes a US$5 option and agrees to sell one Intel stock for $20 on December 1, 2014. Investor A agrees to pay $5 and obtains this stock option. In this example, our option contract has two participants: investor A and investor B, where investor A plays the buyer and investor B plays the call writer. Investor B will be paid $5 and subsequently will provide investor A with the option certificate (the physical asset). The stock option in question (the physical asset) is derived from the stock option asset type, with the specific stock type (the paper asset) being an instrument in the underlying option. In this example, the CONTRACT ASSET ALLOCATION will store and maintain the following two records to account for the above-mentioned facts: the first record will associate investor A (who is the option buyer) with $5 in cash (the amount). The second record will associate investor B (who is the option seller) with the stock option and will set the quantity equal to one. Using these CONTRACT ASSET ALLOCATION records (together with the CONTRACT PARTICIPATION, OPTION EXERCISE SCHEDULE, and ROLE TYPE), you can easily reconstruct the original structure of the option and explain who was responsible for what, as well as the original cost of the given option.

According to the model, the OPTION TYPE is further categorized according to the OPTION STYLE TYPE supertype. Moreover, the OPTION STYLE TYPE supertype is subtyped into items such as:

- AMERICAN (options that may be exercised at any time prior to option expiration)

- EUROPEAN (options that may be exercised only at the expiration date)

- BERMUDAN (similar to an American option in that they may be exercised before the expiration of the option, but similar to a European option in that they may be exercised only on predefined dates)

The Importance of Mathematical Models

Many mathematical models have been developed to explain how to calculate option prices and understand what direction these prices may take in the near (and not so near) future. One of these,—the *Black-Scholes-Merton* model— is widely accepted and extremely popular in academia.[1] The Black-Scholes-Merton model, taught in most MBA programs worldwide, is used to calculate European-style option prices.

---

[1]In 1997, Robert Merton and Myron Scholes received the Nobel Prize for their contribution to economics and financial engineering. (Fischer Black passed away in 1995 and therefore wasn't able to be awarded the Nobel Prize.)

The main assumptions and simplifications used in the Black-Scholes-Merton model are the following:

- An option can be only exercised upon expiration.
- Interest rates are constant.
- Underlying stocks don't pay dividends.
- Future market directions cannot be predicted.
- Commissions are not charged during the transaction.
- Volatility is constant over time.
- Asset price follows a geometric Brownian motion with a constant drift.

Caution The Black-Scholes-Merton assumptions tend to introduce certain inaccuracies into option pricing calculations if not used correctly, and thus may subject traders to excessive risk.

The most significant limitations of the Black-Scholes-Merton model are as follows:

- It produces incorrect results for stocks that pay high dividends.
- In real life, interest rates are never constant.
- Volatility cannot be constant over time.
- The assumption that dividends are only paid upon option expiration is not always plausible.
- The model assumes that large jumps in stock prices do not occur.
- The model cannot correctly predict the true value of American options; it undervalues them due to the following assumption: options can be only exercised upon expiration. American-type options may be exercised at any time prior to the option expiration date.

Despite its limitations, the Black-Scholes-Merton model remains popular in academia and among traders because of its simplicity. Even though the model introduces various inaccuracies in option price calculations, it still produces adequate approximate results if used prudently.

A variation of the Black-Scholes-Merton model is called *autoregressive conditional heteroskedasticity* (ACH). The main assumption under this model is that volatility is not constant but random. Most financial shops have developed their own models, incorporating even more complex models of volatility.

Calculating Volatility from Historical Data

The *volatility* of a stock is a measurement of investor uncertainty (or risk) regarding the stock's future return. Because stock price volatility plays such an important role in options price derivations, we provide an example of a calculation based on historical stock price data. Our assumption is that the stock in question doesn't pay any dividends, as this will help simplify our calculation.

Table 6-1 estimates the volatility of ORCL stock based on the assumption that there are 252 trading days in a year (the closing price data are simulated, even though it is close to the real-life data.) The "day" column specifies when the stock price was observed and the "ORCL Closing Price (USD)" column specifies the closing price (in USD) of the stock on that particular day. In this example, the stock price was observed for 20 consecutive days. The best approach, most practitioners agree, is to calculate stock price volatility on a daily schedule based on closing day prices. According to our sample calculation, the standard deviation of the daily return based on the simulated Oracle closing stock price data between February 20, 2013, and March 20, 2013, is 0.011587 or 1.1587%. Based on this value, the estimated volatility per annum (assuming that there are 252 trading days in a year) is 0.183938 or approximately 18.4%.

Table 6-1. Calculating Volatility from Historical Data

Day	ORCL Closing Price (USD)	Ln(Price/Price-1)	Power(Ln(Price/Price-1),2)
20-Feb-13	35.50		0.000000
21-Feb-13	34.95	-0.015614	0.000244
22-Feb-13	34.51	-0.012669	0.000161
25-Feb-13	35.07	0.016097	0.000259
26-Feb-13	34.28	-0.022784	0.000519
27-Feb-13	34.25	-0.000876	0.000001
28-Feb-13	34.70	0.013053	0.000170
1-Mar-13	34.12	-0.016856	0.000284
4-Mar-13	34.53	0.011945	0.000143
5-Mar-13	35.22	0.019786	0.000391
6-Mar-13	35.50	0.007919	0.000063
7-Mar-13	35.94	0.012318	0.000152
8-Mar-13	35.94	0.000000	0.000000
11-Mar-13	35.70	-0.006700	0.000045
12-Mar-13	35.85	0.004193	0.000018
13-Mar-13	35.82	-0.000837	0.000001
14-Mar-13	35.80	-0.000559	0.000000
15-Mar-13	36.11	0.008622	0.000074
18-Mar-13	36.10	-0.000277	0.000000
19-Mar-13	36.18	0.002214	0.000005
20-Mar-13	35.98	-0.005543	0.000031
	Total	0.013431	0.002560
Number of trading days	20.00		
Standard deviation of the daily return = SQRT(((Number of Days - 1)* 0.002560) - POWER(0.013431,2)/(Number of Days * (Number of Days -1)))	0.011587		
Number of trading days	252.00		
Estimate of volatility per annum = standart deviation of the daily return * SQRT(number of trading days)	0.183938		

As you can see, the calculation of stock price volatility over a specific period of time is relatively straightforward. However, you should keep in mind that as the sample size increases, the computational process becomes more complicated. Most financial shops will perform these types of calculations on numerous stocks over extended periods of time; performance becomes the primary issue.

Option Contract Variable Assignment

Financial analysts are very interested in certain market variables (otherwise known as *measures*) when valuating option contracts and deciding whether to exercise them. A business interested in finding an option's worth will use market variables to perform various statistical calculations. Typically, options are valuated daily and the results of these calculations are stored in a database. For instance, assume that a financial firm owns an American-style option, which can be exercised at any time prior to the maturity of the option contract. These analysts will be interested in knowing whether they should hold on to this particular American option or early-exercise their option to get rid of it on any given day.

Incidentally, a good strategy is to early-exercise an American-style option right before the dividend date. The reason for this is that dividends reduce the intrinsic value of stocks. Once the stock price is expected to go down, the value of the call option is expected to decline. The value of the put option, on the other hand, is expected to increase.

Your organization may favor a specific set of statistical models designed to approximate future option price movements. These models and their underlying formulas depend on a number of market variables. Thus, it is very important to model these variables properly (and by "properly" we mean adding these important variables dynamically, on demand, and without performing much recoding).

Figure 6-7 models the contract VARIABLE ASSIGNMENT and the corresponding SUGGESTED VARIABLE ASSIGNMENT entities, specifically tailored to our option contract type. The SUGGESTED VARIABLE ASSIGNMENT stores and maintains the variables that were assigned on the CONTRACT TYPE level. These data could be suggested by a particular financial organization or by another important ruling body.

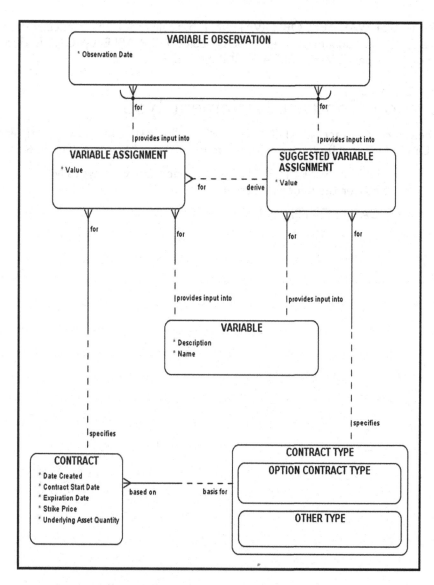

Figure 6-7. Option contract variable assignment

Variables that are stored and maintained on the contract level are, as their name implies, contract-specific. Note that the dependency of the VARIABLE ASSIGNMENT on the SUGGESTED VARIABLE ASSIGNMENT is nonmandatory on both sides. However, you may have to review this relationship and make it mandatory (at least on the VARIABLE ASSIGNMENT side). As is nearly always the case, your underlying business requirements will guide you on how to proceed.

The resulting VARIABLE OBSERVATION (physically made on a particular date) is either based on a more generic SUGGESTED VARIABLE ASSIGNMENT or a contract-specific VARIABLE ASSIGNMENT, but not both.

Option Contract Settlement Type

The option contract SETTLEMENT TYPE explicitly specifies how a particular CONTRACT will be settled, with the following possible values (Figure 6-8):

- PHYSICAL SETTLEMENT, where one party will physically deliver the underlying asset
- CASH SETTLEMENT

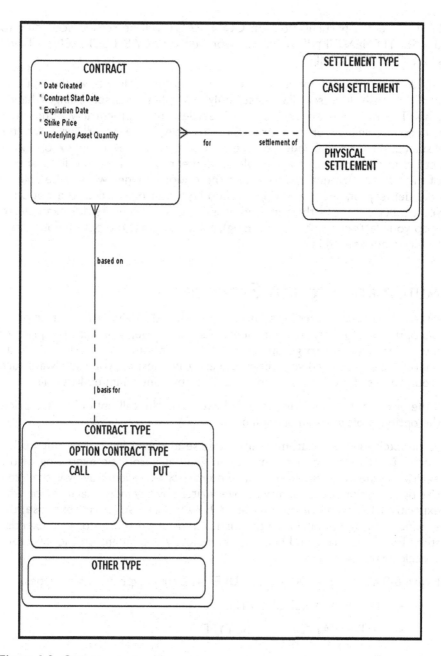

Figure 6-8. Option contract settlement type

In Figure 6-8, a particular option CONTRACT will be settled according to the SETTLEMENT TYPE (which is subtyped into CASH SETTLEMENT and PHYSICAL SETTLEMENT).

Under the cash settlement type, an option holder will receive the option's profit in cash. In cases like these, only one physical asset changes hands: cash. The main reason behind a cash settlement is practicality; sometimes it becomes difficult or even impossible to deliver the underlying asset (for instance, the S&P 500 index options). In fact, almost every index option is settled in cash, making it a valuable settlement type. The main disadvantage of the cash settlement option is that the option's owner will not be able to take delivery on the underlying commodity upon exercise of the option. If you expect to receive the commodity assets out of necessity (for example, to keep your factory machinery running), make sure that the option you intend to buy is not settled in cash.

Automatic Option Exercise

If the price of the underlying asset is higher than the call option's strike price, the option is often called *in the money*. As a call buyer, you want the price of the underlying asset to go up relative to the option's strike price. Once an option is exercised and you obtain the asset in question, you can always turn around and sell it on the spot market, thus obtaining an immediate gain.

If the price of the underlying asset is lower than the call option's strike price, the option is often called *out of money*.

Some exchanges will automatically exercise any expiring call or put option that is $0.01 or more in the money. In general, automatic exercising of the expiring in the money option is called *exercise by exception*. However, the exercise by exception protocol may be overwritten by any individual investor who explicitly instructs his or her broker on how to exercise (or not exercise) the specific expiring option. Once the instructions are made, automatic exercise stops being automatic and becomes completely dependent on the investor's specific instructions.

Figure 6-9 models the EXERCISE RULE TYPE supertype and its subtypes:

- MANUAL EXERCISE TYPE
- AUTOMATIC EXERCISE TYPE.

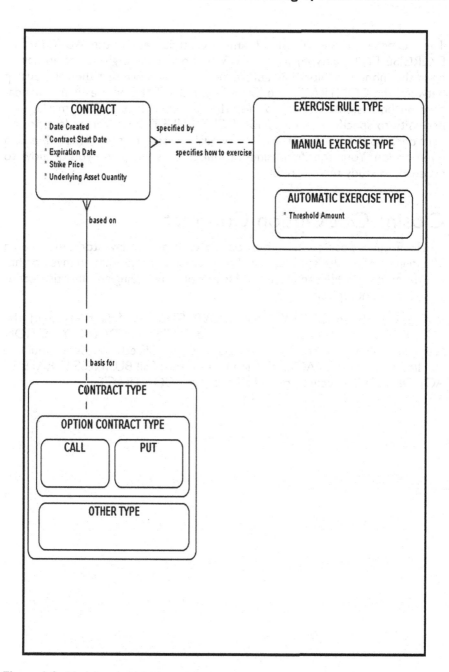

Figure 6-9. Modeling an option's exercise type

The purpose of the threshold amount attribute (of the AUTOMATIC EXERCISE TYPE subtype) is to specify by how much a given option has to be in the money to initiate an automatic exercise. Note that the relationship between the CONTRACT and EXERCISE RULE TYPE entities is nonmandatory on both sides. The reason for this is simple: in the OTC market the necessity to specify the proper EXERCISE RULE TYPE becomes less prominent because the onus is on each individual investor to properly terminate a given option. Your specific business requirements will guide you on how to proceed, so study them carefully.

Closing Out Option Contract

To close out a position in a given option contract, an investor can issue an *offsetting order* on the same option. For example, assume that an investor has bought an option. He can close out his position by issuing an offsetting order to sell the same option.

In Figure 6-10, an OFFSETTING ORDER STRATEGY (a subtype of the BUSINESS STRATEGY) and the associated BUSINESS STRATEGY ACTION ITEMS identify how, according to the business, any offsetting orders should be handled. CONTRACT ACTIVITY identifies a set of all BUSINESS STRATEGY ACTION ITEMS executed on behalf of a given CONTRACT.

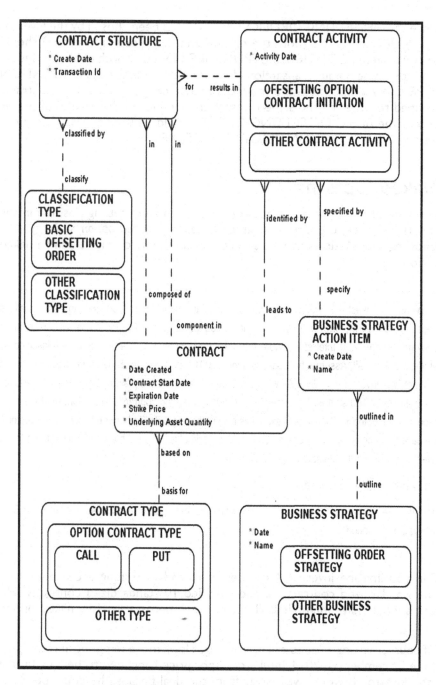

Figure 6-10. Closing out an option contract

Once the OFFSETTING ORDER STRATEGY has been chosen by the investor, the resulting contracts (both the original and the offsetting contract) should be stored in the CONTRACT STRUCTURE. Note that both contracts should share the same unique transaction identifier. Moreover, the CLASSIFICATION TYPE entity should help the modeler further categorize a set of contracts grouped together by the same transaction identifier. In the case of offsetting orders, the BASIC OFFSETTING ORDER should be used to classify the offsetting orders in the CONTRACT STRUCTURE.

Naked Options

When an option contract is not combined with an offsetting position in the underlying stock, the option strategy is called a *naked option* strategy. The following hypothetical example should explain the mechanics behind a naked option.

Example　Investor A writes a European-style call option for US$50 and agrees to sell on December 31, 2014, one Intel option standardized contract for $20 per share, without actually owning the underlying Intel stock. Note that the above-mentioned scenario is often classified as writing a naked call. Assume that today is June 1, 2014, and investor B has purchased the option contract from investor A for $50. As we have already learned, one option contract typically requires the purchase of 100 shares. On December 31, 2014, upon the contract's expiration, the Intel stock price ends up being $25; investor B exercises his purchasing right. To honor this contract, investor A will have to purchase the Intel shares on the spot market for $25 per share and deliver them to the investor B, which will culminate in the following loss:

$$(100 \times (\$25 - \$20)) - \$50 = \$450$$

Note that we subtract $50 because this is the amount that investor A received from investor B for writing the call option.

Can you imagine investor A's losses if, instead of writing a call option on one standardized contract, he had specified 10 standardized contracts? His losses would have multiplied, all due to his unnecessarily risky naked option strategy.

Of course, writing a naked call option might look more tempting in retrospect if the December 31, 2014, Intel stock spot price happened to be $15. In that case, investor B would walk away from the deal because he could purchase the same shares for a lower price on the spot market, allowing investor A to pocket the original option payment of $50. Regardless of the outcome, however, writing a naked call is very risky and frowned on by most regulators.

Let's review the model in Figure 6-10 to see how it can help us identify a naked option strategy. Again, contracts that are part of the same overall strategy should be grouped together by a common transaction identifier and classified according to a common CLASSIFICATION TYPE. Assume that investor A alters his trading strategy and executes the following trading steps:

1. He enters into one December forward contract to purchase 100 Intel shares.

2. He writes a December-expiring call option to sell these 100 Intel shares.

As a result, we would group together the contracts that form the backbone of the trading strategy and allow them to share the same transaction identifier and the same CLASSIFICATION TYPE. Incidentally, the CLASSIFICATION TYPE for this particular trading strategy could be called WRITING A COVERED CALL. By examining the CONTRACT STRUCTURE and the CONTRACT data, we can easily spot anomalous contracts and identify the parties responsible for them.

Modeling an Option's Delivery Subject Area

Figure 6-11 models an option's delivery subject area. Assume that an investor takes a long position in a call option to purchase one share of Microsoft stock. The option in question is targeted for physical settlement and expires on December 31, 2013. Upon the option's expiration, if the market conditions are favorable, the investor will be able to exercise this option. Option exercise, in general, may be considered an *asset-transforming* event. Here, the investor transforms the actual stock option and cash into one Microsoft stock certificate. The main reason for this type of transaction is the investor's intention to keep that specific stock for the long term for speculative purposes.

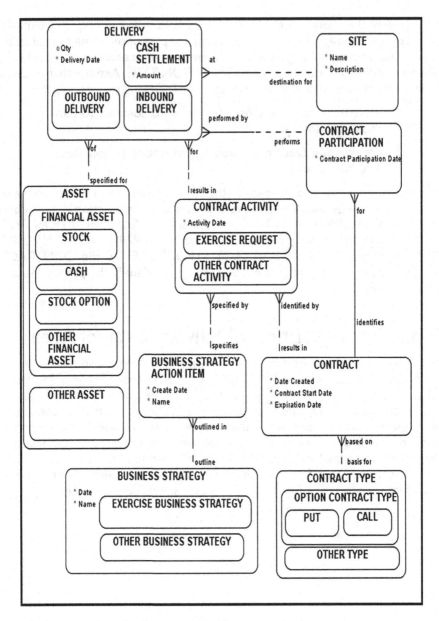

Figure 6-11. Modeling an option contract's delivery

At the end of the transaction, the party who writes the call option will have to deliver the underlying stock (the physical asset). Upon completion of the delivery, the option ceases to exist and the underlying paper asset is transformed into a physical one (the stock certificate).

The model in Figure 6-11 does not reflect certain steps that you, as the modeler, will have to consider. Once delivery is complete, your application logic will have to remove the expired option from your physical asset pool. In a physical database, it is rarely considered preferable to physically delete data; it is generally considered more sensible to flag deleted rows by applying a so-called *soft delete* (aka *logical delete*). Removing one physical asset (the stock option) from the inventory pool and adding another physical asset (the stock) is a process and thus cannot be shown directly in the data model; these tasks must be modeled separately by process architects.

FLEX Options

Flexible exchange-traded options (FLEX) were introduced by the CBOE in 1993. These are option contracts without specifically set terms, meaning that these contracts are nonstandard. Here, one party may set the overall structure of a contract and specify a particular exercise date or strike price. As one could expect, it takes time and effort to find a counterparty who will agree to the structure of the underlying FLEX contract. FLEX contracts take a relatively long time to negotiate and purchase, resulting in their being less liquid compared to standardized option contracts. However, they can be useful for profiting from the OTC option market. Figure 6-12 diagrams one way to model FLEX option contracts.

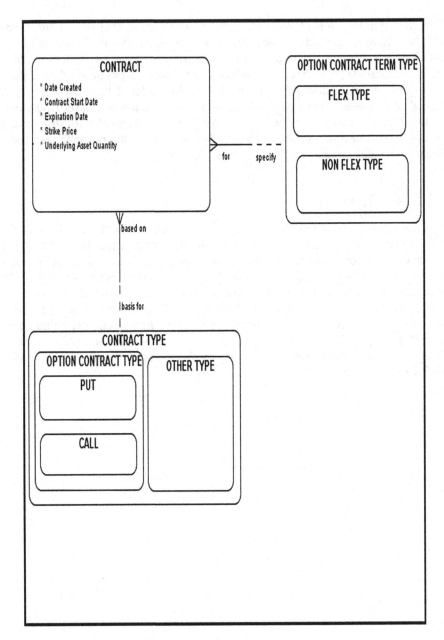

Figure 6-12. Modeling FLEX contract options

Standard option contracts have a set of already defined terms, such as the strike price and expiration date. FLEX option contracts, on the other hand, allow investors to fine-tune the following terms to their specific needs:

- Option contract strike price

- Expiration date

- Option style type (typically American or European)

- Contract size

- Option type (call or put)

- Settlement calculation (which is based either on the opening settlement value or the closing settlement value)

Conclusion

This chapter discussed the option contract basics, studied the underlying business rules, and created various starter data models. The starter models I designed and built in this chapter using familiar building blocks should help you get some insight into the inner workings of option contracts. The next chapter will discuss advanced option trading strategies and ways to model them, gradually expanding our knowledge and reusing the concepts we learned in this chapter.

Modeling Advanced Options Strategies

Cogito, ergo sum.

—René Descartes, *Principia Philosophiae*

This chapter shows how financial engineers combine various contracts to produce unique and useful profit patterns. Previous chapters were primarily concerned with a singular contract, which you learned how to model with the help of specific business rules. This chapter explains the profit patterns and mechanics of compound contracts and demonstrates the ways they can be modeled. The discussion begins with a simple strategy involving one stock and one option.

A Simple Strategy Involving One Stock and One Option

Chapter 6 acquainted you with the dangers of the naked option strategy. Recall that selling a call option on an asset that you don't physically own is called writing a naked call. This risky strategy may backfire, leading to significant losses and damage to the seller's reputation. This section discusses the opposite strategy and ways to protect yourself against the dangers of the naked call.

Consider the following simple example of the strategy of *writing a covered call*, whereby an investor takes a long position in a stock and a short position in a call option.

Example   Assume that investor A simultaneously enters into two contracts. The first contract is a forward contract to buy 100 shares of Oracle stock on November 1, 2014. The second contract is an option contract to sell the same 100 Oracle shares on November 4, 2014. Notice that the expiration dates of these contracts are not exactly the same but are relatively close to each other. Overall, these two contracts will eventually (more or less) offset each other, resulting in a much better risk-management strategy than the naked call.

Careful analysis of this strategy shows that the long position in the stock protects the investor against a stock price hike that would negatively affect the investor's short position in the call option. Do you see why? Assume that an investor sells a call option on one Intel share at US$20. Upon the option's expiration, the investor delivers the Intel share, as promised, even though the Intel spot price on the delivery day is $29. Instead of selling the Intel share on the spot market at a profit, the investor suffers a loss and delivers it to his counterparty for $20. In general, as a call writer, you would want the underlying asset price to go down.

Traders can adopt other payoff patterns involving one stock and one option, including the following:

- Taking a short position in a stock and a long position in a call option (the *reverse of writing a covered call*)

- Purchasing a put option on a stock and the stock itself (sometimes called a *protective put*)

- Taking a short position in a put option and a short position in the stock itself (called the *reverse of a protective put*)

To model these four alternatives, the trading CLASSIFICATION TYPE super-type is widened to include the following subtypes:

- WRITING A COVERED CALL
- REVERSE OF WRITING A COVERED CALL
- PROTECTIVE PUT
- REVERSE OF A PROTECTIVE PUT

These subtypes enable the modeler to properly classify and group a particular trading strategy and identify each physical contract forming the backbone of a specific trading strategy.

The diagram in Figure 7-1 illustrates the expansion of an already familiar CLASSIFICATION TYPE supertype.

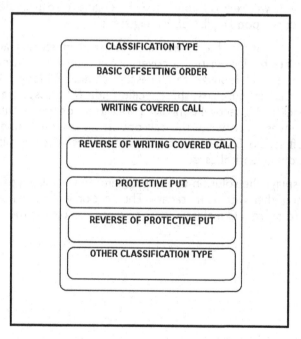

CLASSIFICATION TYPE

- BASIC OFFSETTING ORDER
- WRITING COVERED CALL
- REVERSE OF WRITING COVERED CALL
- PROTECTIVE PUT
- REVERSE OF PROTECTIVE PUT
- OTHER CLASSIFICATION TYPE

Figure 7-1. Expanding the CLASSIFICATION TYPE supertype

Note that each trading strategy mentioned above can easily be accommodated by the CONTRACT STRUCTURE (Figure 7.4).

Option Strategy Metadata Modeling

This section detours from payoff profit patterns to discuss *metadata modeling*. Such models allow us the ability to describe, store, and maintain the data behind a particular trading strategy. Once you understand how to model trading strategy metadata, you should be able to apply these principles and shape and mold them according to your specific business requirements.

Let's assume you are working with a financial engineer who has asked you to come up with some data structures that will allow him to store and maintain a particular trading strategy, along with the corresponding business steps required to carry it out. Eventually these structures may develop into a library of all of the company-wide preapproved trading strategies coupled with their corresponding trading steps. Before you start modeling *metadata*—data that describe other data—you need to understand the underlying business steps. In this case, you will rely on your financial engineer to provide the trading strategy and corresponding list of trading steps.

Assume that the financial engineer is interested in storing and maintaining the metadata behind writing a covered call. The first contract (the long position in the stock) requires the investor to take the long position in the forward contract to purchase the specific underlying asset (say, a share of Microsoft stock). The second contract (the short position in the call option) requires the investor to write the call option on the same underlying asset (the Microsoft stock). Both contracts should have relatively similar expiration dates and involve identical assets.

Figure 7-2 displays the solution to the problem of modeling a particular trading strategy together with its metadata. This section examines how this model enables you to store and maintain your covered call option metadata.

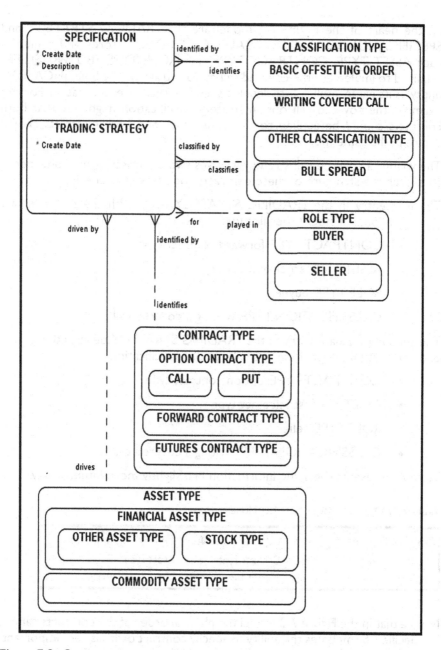

Figure 7-2. Option strategy metadata modeling

At the heart of the Figure 7-2 model are the TRADING STRATEGY and SPECIFICATION entities. The TRADING STRATEGY stores and maintains each ASSET TYPE, CONTRACT TYPE, and ROLE TYPE (BUYER/SELLER) required to implement the covered call option strategy. The SPECIFICATION entity, as its name implies, lists detailed specifications for each strategy. For this example, the covered call option strategy specification might say that both contracts should be applied to the same stock and both contracts should expire in the same month.

The writing a covered call strategy involves two contracts; your model needs to explain the structure of these contracts and associated entities.

The first entry in the TRADING STRATEGY deals with the first contract (long position in a stock) specification:

- CONTRACT TYPE: forward contract type

- ASSET TYPE: stock asset type

- ROLE TYPE: buyer

- CLASSIFICATION TYPE: writing a covered call

The second metadata entry in the TRADING STRATEGY deals with the second contract (short position in a call option) specification:

- CONTRACT TYPE: option contract type

- ASSET TYPE: stock asset type

- ROLE TYPE: seller

- CLASSIFICATION TYPE: writing a covered call

Table 7-1 presents the same information in a slightly more intuitive way.

Table 7-1. Option Strategy Metadata Modeling

Classification Type	Contract Type	Asset Type	Role Type
Writing a covered call	Forward Contract Type	Stock Asset Type	Buyer
Writing a covered call	Option Contract Type	Stock Asset Type	Seller

Notice that in the Figure 7-2 model the physical order of the contracts cannot be specified. Sometimes the ability to specify contract order is very important. To incorporate this requirement, you can add the order identifier attribute to the TRADING STRATEGY entity. This attribute (and eventually column) will specify the physical order of the records in the TRADING STRATEGY.

Note that the diagram in Figure 7-2 deals only with types. This is done by design; in metadata modeling, your job is to explain the internal constitution of the metadata in terms of types (or blueprints) rather than in terms of the actual embodiment of these types. The Figure 7-2 model accommodates the more complex scenarios developed in the following sections.

Bull Spreads

If an investor feels that the price of a particular stock will rise modestly in the time span between time 1 and time 2, he may choose to implement a *bull spread strategy.* This strategy allows the investor to make a small profit when market conditions become favorable and protects him against excessive losses when conditions become unfavorable, thus limiting risk. For instance, an investor who has a call option with the strike price S1 might decide to give up potential future profit if the price increases to S2 to limit his risk.

A bull spread strategy is executed by the following steps:

1. Buying a call option on a stock with a certain strike price (S1)

2. Selling a call option on the same stock with a higher strike price (S2, where S2 > S1). The hope here is that the stock price will go up during this time.

3. Both options expiring in the same month.

To accommodate the bull spread strategy to the Figure 7-2 data model, focus on the business rule specifying that the strike price S2 must be greater than the strike price S1 and that the options under consideration should expire in the same month. This business rule is our bull spread SPECIFICATION.

The first metadata entry in the TRADING STRATEGY deals with the first contract metadata specification:

- CONTRACT TYPE: call

- ASSET TYPE: stock option asset type

- ROLE TYPE: buyer

- CLASSIFICATION TYPE: bull spread

The second **en**try in the TRADING STRATEGY deals with the second contract specification:

- CONTRACT TYPE: call

- ASSET TYPE: stock option asset type

- ROLE TYPE: seller

- CLASSIFICATION TYPE: bull spread

By following the same overall pattern, we can specify any trading strategy, including *bear spreads*, discussed in the next section.

Bear Spreads

If an investor anticipates that a particular stock price will go down, but not by much, he or she may choose to pursue a *bear spread strategy*. This strategy is executed through the following steps:

1. Buying a put option at a certain strike price (S1)

2. Selling a put option with another strike price (S2), where S1 > S2

3. Both options expiring in the same month.

Here, the investor purchases the put option with the strike price S1 and decides to give up any potential profit at price S2, resulting in an intricately constructed mechanism designed to protect against excessive risk exposure. For this strategy to function properly, both contracts need to expire in the same month.

The business rule specifying that the strike price S1 has to be greater than S2 and that both contracts should expire in the same month is the bear spread SPECIFICATION.

The first metadata entry in the TRADING STRATEGY deals with the first contract metadata specification:

- CONTRACT TYPE: put

- ASSET TYPE: stock option asset type

- ROLE TYPE: buyer

- CLASSIFICATION TYPE: BEAR SPREAD

The second entry in the TRADING STRATEGY deals with the second contract specification:

- CONTRACT TYPE: put

- ASSET TYPE: stock option asset type

- ROLE TYPE: seller

- CLASSIFICATION TYPE: BEAR SPREAD

In Figure 7-3, the CLASSIFICATION TYPE supertype is widened by the addition of the BEAR SPREAD subtype.

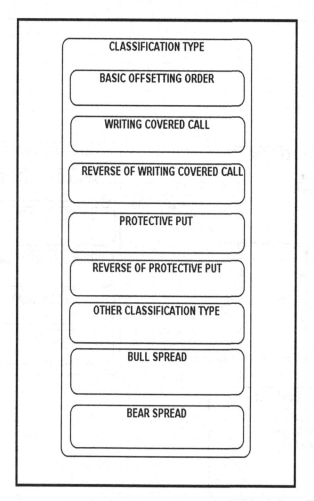

Figure 7-3. Extending the CLASSIFICATION TYPE and introducing the BEAR SPREAD subtype

Revisiting the Contract Structure Entity

As you know, the main purpose of the CONTRACT STRUCTURE and CLASSIFICATION TYPE entities is to assemble a pattern out of a collection of seemingly dispersed contracts (see Figure 7-4). You can easily query these two tables and retrieve the contracts that form the backbone of a particular trading strategy. By examining these contracts, you can determine:

- Where you stand in terms of execution of a specific trading strategy
- What work still needs to be done
- Whether any of the required offsetting contracts is absent

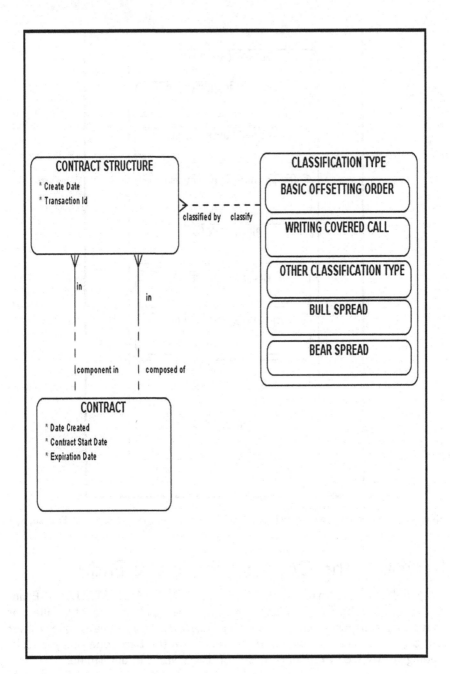

Figure 7-4. Revisiting contract structure

For instance, you expect to find two contracts in the CONTRACT STRUCTURE to account for a particular BULL SPREAD trading strategy. Any deviation from the expected results would be reason to investigate the data in question.

In fact, by running queries against the CONTRACT STRUCTURE (and associated entities) you can perform various data forensics and can easily spot data anomalies related to a specific trading strategy. Once you spot data anomalies in the CONTRACT STRUCTURE, it is a relatively straightforward process to obtain the detailed information regarding who might be responsible for the questionable contracts. How do we do that? CONTRACT PARTICIPATION is a good place to start.

The diagram in Figure 7-5 ties together the by now familiar concepts of CONTRACT, CONTRACT STRUCTURE, and CONTRACT PARTICIPATION, enabling you to answer a variety of questions related to a particular CONTRACT, including those related to contract delivery, contract participation, and various other contract activities.

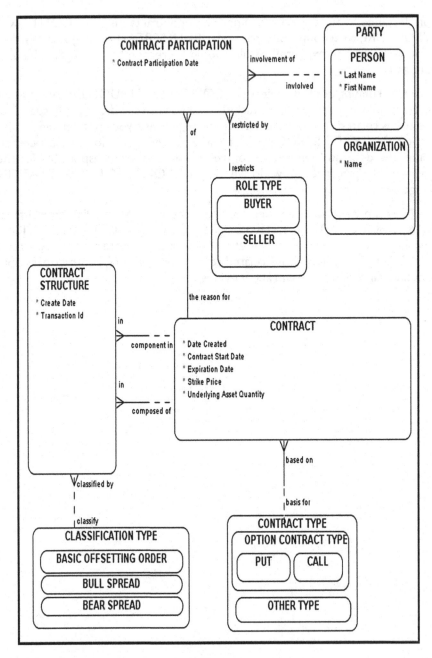

Figure 7-5. Tying together contract participation and contract structure

Conclusion

This chapter showed the application of many concepts you learned in previous chapters to the practical tasks of modeling how financial engineers combine various contracts to produce unique and useful profit patterns. I urge you to practice as many data modeling tasks as possible. After all, practice makes perfect. A systematic application of your newly learned concepts will guarantee you success and recognition. Passive learning guarantees you nothing.

Recommended Reading

Robert L. McDonald, *Derivatives Markets*, 3rd ed. Prentice Hall, 2009.

Swaps and Forward Rate Agreements

An optimist may see a light where there is none, but why must the pessimist always run to blow it out?

—Michel de Saint-Pierre

Swap contracts and forward rate contracts play prominent roles in the OTC derivatives market. This chapter follows the now-familiar pattern by defining each contract type, explaining its underlying business rules, and then proceeding to model it.

Defining a Swap

A *swap contract* is an agreement to exchange cash flows at some time in the future, according to a predetermined schedule. The agreement specifies the cash flow exchange dates and the cash flow calculation method.

The forward contract, discussed in Chapter 4, is an example of a simple swap contract. Consider the following hypothetical case: company A enters into a forward contract with company B to buy 200 ounces of copper at US$50 per ounce on December 31, 2014. The contract start date is December 31, 2013. At the expiration date of this contract (December 31, 2014), company

A will receive from company B 200 ounces of copper and will pay $10,000 (200 × $50).

One strategy available to company A is to sell the copper right away at the spot price of copper on that particular day. The loss or profit will be dictated by the spot price of copper on that day. In actuality, however, the delivery mechanism of the forward contract will be simplified, resulting in a cash settlement in which the total quantity of copper (200 ounces) will be multiplied by the difference between the copper's spot price and the contract's underlying forward price ($50 per ounce). Take note: cash flow exchanges occur only once, at the expiration date of the forward contract.

Swap contracts, on the other hand, result in an exchange of cash flows on a number of predefined dates. The two most popular swap contract types are:

- Plain vanilla interest rate swaps
- Fixed-for-fixed currency rate swaps

Plain Vanilla Interest Rate Swaps

A simple example illustrates how a *plain vanilla interest rate swap* contract works.

Example Assume that company A has US$10,000 to invest and the current interest rate is 4 percent. Company A's treasurer may feel that the interest rate will fall in the near future and thus might agree to exchange cash flows with company B, according to the following schedule:

Every six months for a period of two years, company A will pay interest at a floating rate and company B will pay interest at a fixed rate (say, 3.8 percent) on the same notional principal ($10,000). Semi-annual payments, for a period of two years, will lead to four payment exchanges.

Typically, the rate in plain vanilla interest rate swaps is the LIBOR. Table 8-1 shows a hypothetical schedule of payments for the example, together with the payment inflow and outflow. Note that during the course of a swap contract, a fixed interest rate always remains the same.

Table 8-1. Hypothetical Schedule of Payments

Notional Principle	Payment Date	Fixed Rate	LIBOR Rate	Floating Cash Outflow	Fixed Cash Inflow
$10,000	Dec. 31, 2013	3.80%			
$10,000	June 31, 2014	3.80%	4.00%	$400	$380
$10,000	Dec. 31, 2014	3.80%	4.10%	$410	$380
$10,000	June 31, 2015	3.80%	3.78%	$378	$380
$10,000	Dec. 31, 2015	3.80%	3.67%	$367	$380

Fixed-for-Fixed Currency Rate Swaps

Fixed-for-fixed currency rate swaps are in effect mechanisms for transforming an investment in one country into an investment in another country. They are best explained by a hypothetical example.

■ **Example**   Consider a company A that feels that the value of the US dollar will strengthen against the British pound (GBP) and consequently invests in US dollars. Company B feels the opposite and invests in GBP. Also, assume that company A is a US-based company and company B is UK-based. These two companies could agree on a principal amount (say, 8 million GBP and US$15 million) and pay each other the fixed amount (hence the term *fixed-for-fixed*) on a predefined schedule. In our case, company A would receive 8 million GBP and pay out a fixed 5 percent rate of interest. Company B would receive US$15 million and agree to pay 4.5 percent interest off this principal amount. At the end of the fixed-for-fixed currency rate swap, the principal amounts plus the remaining cash flows would be exchanged.

Fixed-for-fixed currency rate swaps help companies better manage their exposure to fluctuations in interest rates and secure better interest rates by leveraging the interest-rate advantage that domestic firms usually have over foreign firms.

International Swaps and Derivative Organization

The document that forms the basis of a swap contract is called a *confirmation*. The standard *confirmation agreement* was designed by the International Swap and Derivative Organization (ISDA, www.isda.org), and this confirmation forms the backbone of every swap agreement in the OTC market. Confirmation agreements and their structure are discussed in the "Modeling ISDA Documentation and Confirmations" section.

Subtyping the Swap Agreement Type

Begin your swap contract modeling task with a relatively simple exercise: properly subtyping (and thus widening) the CONTRACT TYPE to account for the SWAP CONTRACT TYPE. As you've already learned, a SWAP CONTRACT TYPE can be further subtyped into a FIXED-FOR-FIXED CURRENCY RATE SWAP TYPE and a PLAIN VANILLA INTEREST RATE SWAP TYPE (Figure 8-1), thus deepening your CONTRACT TYPE hierarchy structure. The model may look simple, but it will give you a significant advantage later on. By linking the CONTRACT to the specific CONTRACT TYPE, you allow the contract to inherit specific business rules that your users will understand and appreciate.

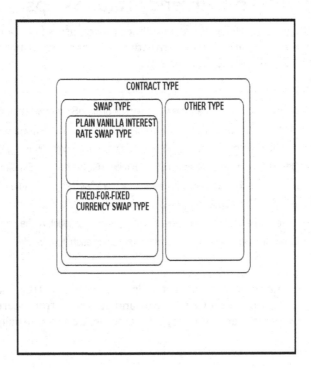

Figure 8-1. Subtyping a contract into a swap type

Interest Rate and Interest Rate Type

The discussion of option contract valuations in Chapter 6 treated the LIBOR (London Interbank Offered Rate) rate as a variable. In this section we deviate from that approach and explicitly create INTEREST RATE and INTEREST RATE TYPE entities. The INTEREST RATE TYPE will be further subtyped into the LIBOR RATE TYPE and the RISK FREE RATE TYPE (Figure 8-2). The INTEREST RATE TYPE represents a rate type that a particular organization may trade in and should be treated as a general blueprint. INTEREST RATE, on the other hand, is the actual interest rate observed on a particular day. The reason these entities are modeled explicitly is because under a swap contract it is of paramount importance to be able to specify clearly which interest rate a particular PARTY in a given CONTRACT is responsible for.

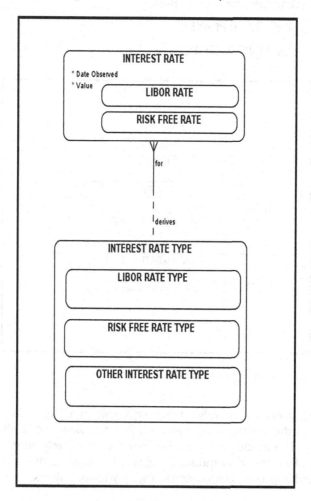

Figure 8-2. Interest rate and interest rate type

At this point you have seen two approaches that deal with interest rate maintenance and tracking. In the previous chapters you've learned how to accomplish such a task by using dynamic variables. This section shows you how to implement the same functionality with the use of INTEREST RATE and INTEREST RATE TYPE entities. The entity approach is more explicit, direct, and easy to understand. However, implementation through the use of variables can be an excellent solution when you don't want to hard-code something and you need a more flexible and dynamic approach.

Fixed and Floating Rate Player Roles

The foregoing discussion of swap contracts introduces two new ROLE TYPES into our modeling toolbox (Figure 8-3):

- A FIXED RATE PLAYER
- A FLOATING RATE PLAYER

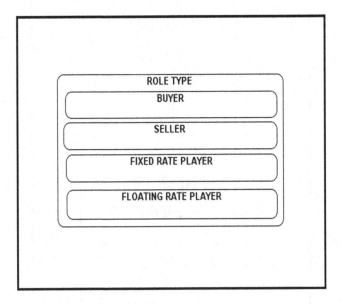

Figure 8-3. Fixed and floating rate player roles

Being able to precisely identify each party's role in a given swap contract is essential from the business requirement's point of view and is often a technical necessity. The model in Figure 8-3 may look relatively simple, but within the context of a larger data model it will better articulate the underlying business rules and improve communication with your end users.

Modeling Swap Contract Participation

Figure 8-4 diagrams the swap contract's participation subject area. To keep the starting model simple and focused, ROLE TYPE is subtyped into only:

- A FIXED RATE PLAYER
- A FLOATING RATE PLAYER

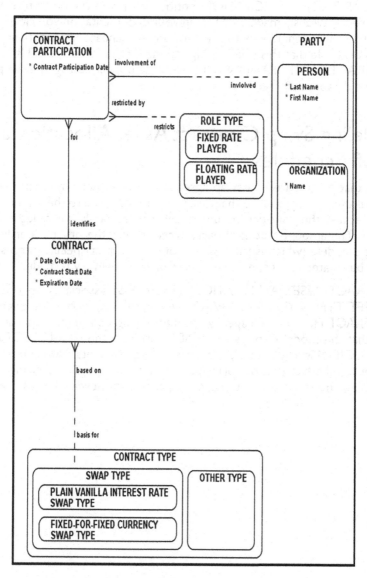

Figure 8-4. Modeling swap contract participation

The BUYER and SELLER subtypes are removed deliberately, because these role types are not applicable to our current situation.

FIXED-FOR-FIXED CURRENCY SWAP TYPE contracts involve at least two participants, each playing a FIXED RATE PLAYER role. PLAIN VANILLA INTEREST RATE SWAP TYPE contracts, on the other hand, involve at least two contract participants, each playing either a FIXED RATE PLAYER role or a FLOATING RATE PLAYER role. The relationship between the CONTRACT and CONTRACT PARTICIPATION entities is mandatory on both sides. As mentioned previously, make sure that in your documentation you clearly specify the reasoning behind why the relationship is mandatory on both sides and the business rule that this relationship attempts to enforce. CONTRACT and CONTRACT PARTICIPATION will have to be populated together as part of the same database transaction.

Modeling Swap Contract Asset Allocation and Payoff Schedules

Parties that participate in a swap agreement may either physically exchange principal amounts (a practice that rarely occurs) or agree to these amounts on paper. Because the principal amount rarely changes hands, it is called a *notional principal*. The amount that each party agrees to pay the other according to a specific schedule (which is the function of the contract-specific interest rate) should be treated as a paper asset unless physical delivery is made.

CONTRACT ASSET ALLOCATION (Figure 8-5) associates an ASSET or an ASSET TYPE with a given PARTY within the context of a given swap CONTRACT. Here we will specify the mutually agreed-on principal amounts. Note that the model displays the ASSET entity on the CONTRACT ASSET ALLOCATION level because your business requirements may require you to account for the fact that the principal amounts may physically change hands. Remember, though, that a notional principal amount never changes hands.

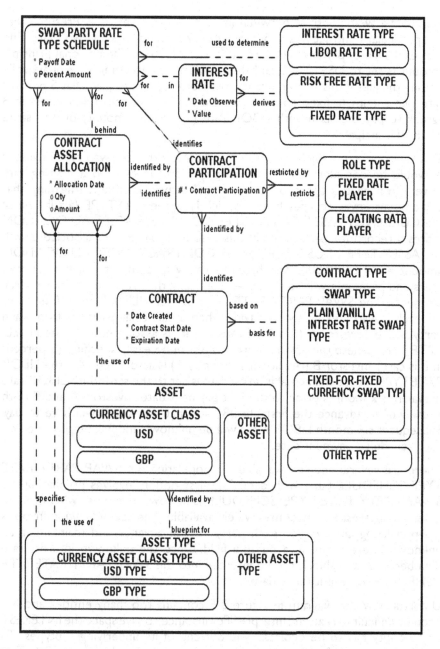

Figure 8-5. Modeling a swap contract asset allocation and payoff schedule (full version)

Consider a swap contract between investor A and investor B. Presume that this particular contract was signed on July 1, 2013, and lasts for two years. The first exchange of payments occurs on January 1, 2014. The notional principal amount is set to US$10,000, and the payments are exchanged semi-annually. During the life of this swap contract, investor A agrees to pay a flat 5 percent rate per annum (a fixed amount) on the notional principal and investor B agrees to pay the six-month LIBOR rate (a variable amount) on the same notional principal.

This contract is classified as a plain vanilla interest rate swap type. Investor A would be considered a fixed rate player and investor B a floating rate player. Both parties agree on the notional principal amount (meaning that this amount never changes hands), which is of the USD TYPE (a subtype of the CURRENCY ASSET CLASS TYPE). CONTRACT ASSET ALLOCATION stores a record for each party; in this case both parties are associated with the ASSET TYPE of USD TYPE and a CONTRACT ASSET ALLOCATION amount equal to 10,000. The hypothetical swap contract will last for two years and payments will be made semi-annually, thus resulting in four overall payments. The SWAP PARTY RATE TYPE SCHEDULE will store four rows for each investor, explicitly specifying when a particular payment from each party is due. Investor A (the fixed rate player) is associated with the FIXED RATE TYPE, where the actual interest rate can be easily specified (5 percent in this case). Investor B (the floating rate player) is associated with the LIBOR RATE TYPE, where the actual interest rate is set to the six-month LIBOR rate prevalent six months prior to the first payment date. Investors A and B both know well in advance the first LIBOR rate that investor B will have to pay. Subsequent six-month LIBOR rates will be unknown and will be observed on each scheduled payment date.

There are several choices available for populating the SWAP PARTY RATE TYPE SCHEDULE table with data. The first option involves populating the SWAP PARTY RATE TYPE SCHEDULE one row at a time, whenever an unknown interest rate becomes widely available. The second option involves pre-populating all rows for each party well in advance and maintaining an unknown interest rate in a nullable field. Once the unknown interest rate data becomes available, it can be inserted into the SWAP PARTY RATE TYPE SCHEDULE to keep it up to date.

Unfortunately, the diagram in Figure 8-5 contains too many entities and has become difficult to read and interpret. For instance, to save space the INTEREST RATE entity has to be depicted without any of its underlying subtypes. To rectify this, a simplified version of this model is displayed in Figure 8-6. This new diagram makes things clearer and less ambiguous because it contains fewer entities.

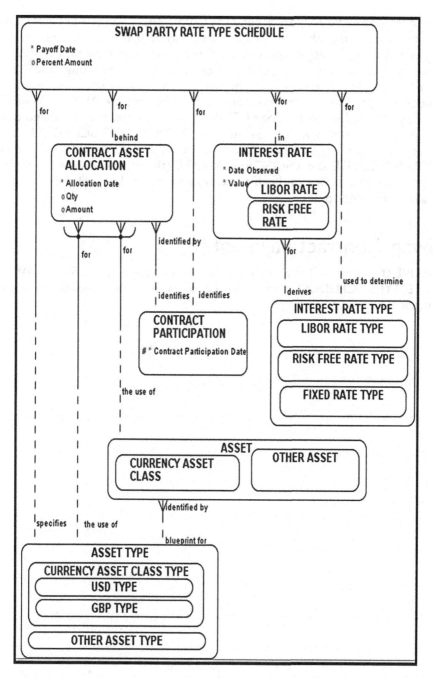

Figure 8-6. Modeling a swap contract asset allocation and payoff schedule (simplified version)

Note that the exclusivity arc around the CONTRACT ASSET ALLOCATION entity indicates that the principal amounts may actually change hands. Once again, this doesn't happen very often. If, per your underlying business rules, you don't expect this to happen, you can simplify the resulting model and remove the ASSET entity (and the associated relationships). Additionally, notice the presence of the relationship between the SWAP PARTY RATE TYPE SCHEDULE and the ASSET TYPE; it indicates that the scheduled payments (implemented via the SWAP PARTY RATE TYPE SCHEDULE) are treated as paper assets. The relationship between the SWAP PARTY RATE TYPE SCHEDULE and the INTEREST RATE (the actual observed interest rate) is nonmandatory on both sides because these data will only become available at a later point.

Swap Contract Payments

DELIVERY (Figure 8-7) in a swap contract is controlled by the SWAP PARTY RATE TYPE SCHEDULE and is associated with physical assets (cash, for instance).

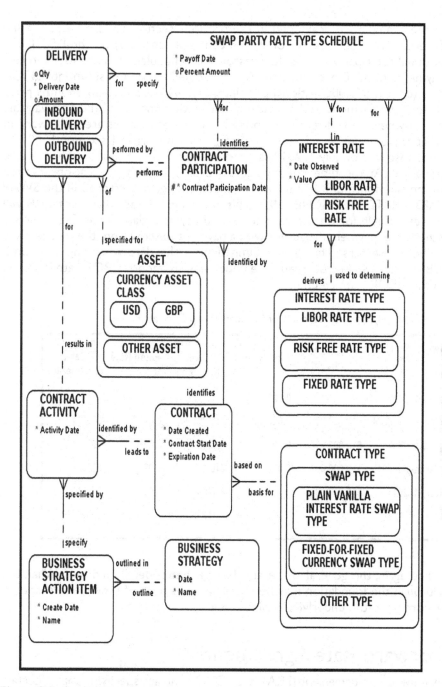

Figure 8-7. Swap contract payments

In the example we developed in the previous section, investor A pays a flat 5 percent rate per annum (or 2.5 percent semi-annually) on the US$10,000 notional principal. As a result, investor A is scheduled to make four interest payments of $250 each. Investor B is scheduled to pay the six-month LIBOR rate (on the $10,000 notional principal) that was observed six months prior to the first payment exchange date. Hence, the amount of the first variable rate payment shouldn't be a surprise because both parties are well aware of what the amount should be. Assuming that the original six-month LIBOR rate, observed on July 1, 2013, is 2.6 percent, investor B will be scheduled to pay $260. At the time the payments are exchanged, a physical observation of the six-month LIBOR rate will be made and its value stored in the SWAP PARTY RATE TYPE SCHEDULE. This is the LIBOR rate that investor B will be responsible for on the next scheduled payment date. Table 8-2 depicts a schedule of payments, together with a payment outflow from the perspectives of both investors. The date column depicts the date when the six-month LIBOR rate will be observed. The underlying six-month LIBOR rate is stored in the LIBOR Rate column.

Table 8-2. Hypothetical Schedule of Payments (Swap Contract Payments)

Date	Principle Amount	LIBOR Rate	Investor B Cash Payments	Fixed Rate	Investor A Cash Payments
July 1, 2013		0.026			
January 1, 2014	$10,000.00	0.028	-260.00	0.025	-250.00
July 1, 2014	$10,000.00	0.024	-280.00	0.025	-250.00
January 1, 2015	$10,000.00	0.023	-240.00	0.025	-250.00
July 1, 2015	$10,000.00		-230.00	0.025	-250.00
		Total:	-1,010.00		-1,000.00

Once again, the general shape and feel of the model should be familiar, but although the foundation may be the same, take note of how we've shaped it according to the underlying business rules.

Forward Rate Agreements

A *forward rate agreement* (FRA) is an OTC contract specifying that a certain interest rate will be applied either to the borrowing or lending of a certain principal amount at some point in the future. The main assumption is that the borrowing or lending is done at the LIBOR rate. The principal amounts are specified on paper and rarely exchanged, thus becoming notional principal amounts. A hypothetical example will clarify the principles underlying a FRA.

Example   Assume that investor A agrees to pay investor B an interest rate of Int_A percent on a principal amount P between times T1 and T2, where T1 and T2 are both dates in the future. Investor B agrees to pay investor A the interest rate of Int_B percent on the same principal amount P between T1 and T2. Assuming that Int_A percent is the LIBOR rate, you can see that an FRA is a perfect tool to hedge against LIBOR rate exposure. Time T1 will be set well in advance, and the time span between T1 and T2 will be clearly specified. Payoff typically will occur at the time T1, when the forward LIBOR rate underlying the time span between T1 and T2 becomes well known, with the payment discounted from the time T2 to T1.

As you can see, the concepts behind an FRA are similar to those behind a swap contract, with the only difference being that an FRA cash flow exchange occurs only once.

FRA Contract Type

The first task related to FRA contract modeling is to define the FRA CONTRACT TYPE and unambiguously show it in the model (Figure 8-8). To keep things simple, the CONTRACT TYPE is subtyped into:

- A FORWARD RATE AGREEMENT TYPE
- OTHER TYPE

Remember that once you relate your contract to a particular contract type, you allow it to inherit specific business rules unique to this particular type. It may seem superfluous at this point, but within the context of a larger data model this subtyping improves communication and removes unnecessary ambiguities.

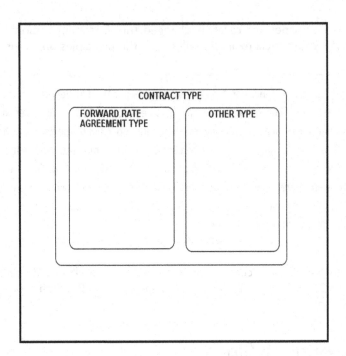

Figure 8-8. Subtyping contract type to account for an FRA contract type

Modeling FRA Contract Participation

An FRA involves a fixed rate player who pays a fixed interest rate between times T1 and T2, and a floating rate player who pays a market realized interest rate (presumably the LIBOR rate) between times T1 and T2 (Figure 8-9). The model in Figure 8-9 looks similar to the swap contract participation diagram in Figure 8-4. This similarity exemplifies how readily you can create something new by understanding the underlying business rules of a contract and combining them with your knowledge of contract modeling in general. Note that the relationship between the CONTRACT and the CONTRACT PARTICIPATION is mandatory on both sides.

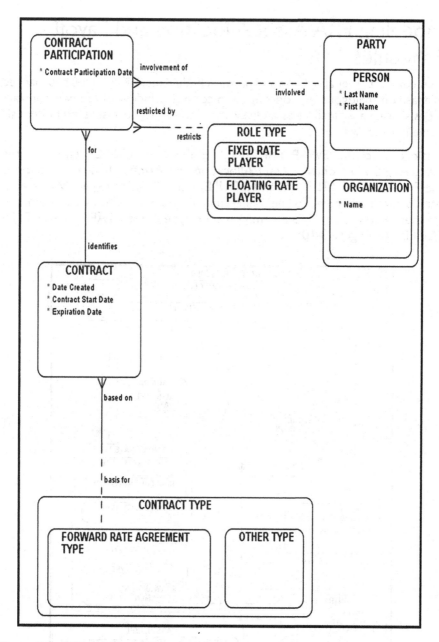

Figure 8-9. FRA contract participation

Modeling FRA Asset Allocation and Payoff Schedules

FRA contract asset allocation and payoff schedule modeling can be approached in a fashion analogous to modeling swap contracts. Indeed, these two contract types share many similarities, and several of the concepts discussed previously serve here as well.

Analogous to the SWAP PARTY RATE TYPE SCHEDULE entity in the "Modeling Swap Contract Asset Allocation and Payoff Schedules" section is the FRA PARTY RATE TYPE SCHEDULE, which likewise explicitly lists each party's payoff schedule. To keep things unambiguous and clear, we can generalize these two entities into a common supertype called a PARTY RATE TYPE SCHEDULE (Figure 8-10).

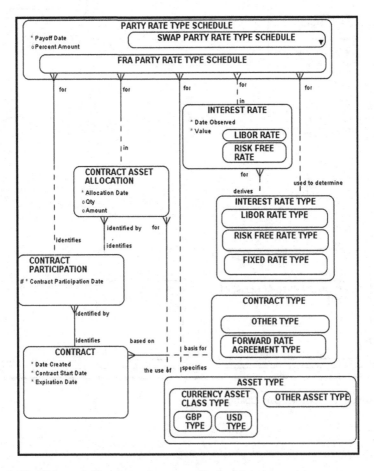

Figure 8-10. FRA asset allocation and rate payoff schedule

The principal amounts underlying a specific FRA contract rarely change hands. To keep our resulting model simple, we state that under the FRA contract the principal amounts never change hands, and thus are notional principal amounts. This simplification results in removing the physical assets from the resulting contract asset allocation model. A hypothetical example will clarify how to use our model in Figure 8-9.

■ **Example**   Assume that investor A, a fixed rate player, has agreed to pay a fixed 5 percent rate on a US$10,000 notional principal amount. This FRA contract is signed on May 1, 2014, with a future start date set to July 1, 2015 (time T1), and a future end date set to January 2, 2016 (time T2). Investor B (the floating rate player) has agreed to pay the market-realized six-month LIBOR rate between July 1, 2015 (T1), and January 1, 2016 (T2) on the $10,000 notional principal. The actual payoff will occur on July 1, 2015 (time T1), once the six-month LIBOR rate covering the time periods between T1 and T2 becomes available. To account for these facts, we begin by populating the CONTRACT ASSET ALLOCATION. The underlying assets in question are paper assets (the notional principal amounts), and that is why we relate the CONTRACT ASSET ALLOCATION to the ASSET TYPE. Mutually agreed-on notional principal amounts are quoted in US dollars, so the ASSET TYPE is specified as a USD TYPE. As a result, you store and maintain two records in the CONTRACT ASSET ALLOCATION (or one CONTRACT ASSET ALLOCATION record per investor).

Once you've populated the CONTRACT ASSET ALLOCATION, you need to account for the actual payoff schedule. Even though an FRA contract only involves one payoff date, it is modeled similarly to the corresponding SWAP PAYOFF SCHEDULE. The FRA PARTY RATE TYPE SCHEDULE stores and maintains a payoff schedule date for each investor. The actual six-month LIBOR rate applicable between times T1 and T2 will be stored whenever this value becomes available, with the payoff date set to the time T1.

Modeling FRA Asset Delivery

An entity that controls an actual FRA contract delivery is a FRA PARTY RATE TYPE SCHEDULE (Figure 8-11). Before the cash flows behind a given FRA contract are exchanged, an interest rate observation must take place. The applicable LIBOR rate must be recorded in the FRA PARTY RATE TYPE SCHEDULE so that the actual payoff amount can be determined. During the delivery phase, physical assets (such as cash) are exchanged between the contract participants; hence, a relationship is established between the DELIVERY entity and the physical ASSET.

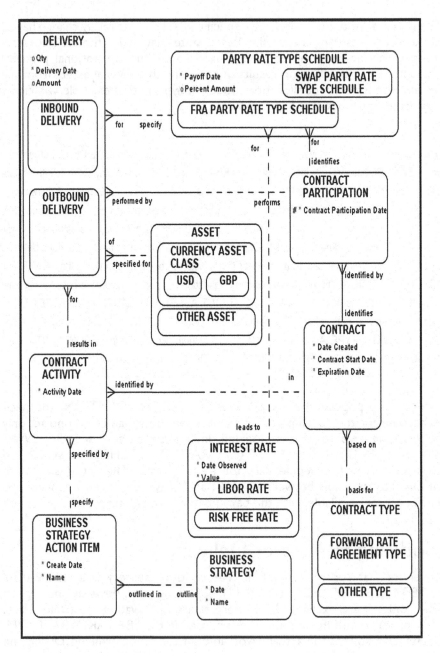

Figure 8-11. FRA and asset delivery

Modeling ISDA Documentation and Confirmations

Most derivative contracts (including swaps and FRAs) in the OTC market are based on the ISDA documentation. ISDA documentation is extremely complex and technical. The reason for this complexity is the necessity of accounting for the underlying contractual risk in the OTC market. In this section we examine the structure of the ISDA documentation and identify its major components.[1]

The main component of the ISDA documentation is the ISDA MASTER AGREEMENT (Figure 8-12). Once the parties sign this agreement, it will govern all future transactions between them. ISDA master agreements can be classified into two types: MULTICURRENCY CROSS BORDER MASTER AGREEMENTS and the LOCAL CURRENCY SINGLE JURISDICTION MASTER AGREEMENTS.

- MULTICURRENCY CROSS BORDER MASTER AGREEMENTS deal with parties located in different jurisdictions, where transactions typically involve different currencies.

- LOCAL CURRENCY SINGLE JURISDICTION MASTER AGREEMENTS deal with parties located in the same jurisdiction, where transactions typically involve the same currency.

---

[1]Tan Sin Liang, *"Documentation of Over-the-Counter Derivatives"* (2001), http://www.lawgazette.com.sg/2001-4/April01-focus.htm.

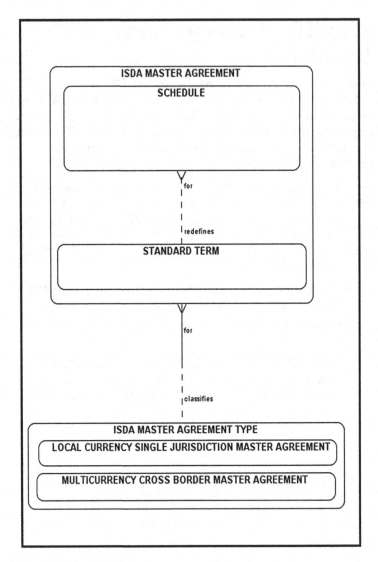

Figure 8-12. Modeling an ISDA document structure

An ISDA MASTER AGREEMENT consists of two sections: the STANDARD TERMS and the SCHEDULE. The STANDARD TERMS deal with things such as netting, events of default, early termination, governing laws, and so forth. These are the standard terms and definitions meant to be negotiated and agreed on by both parties. The SCHEDULE section references the standard terms and their agreed-on definitions. In addition, the schedule lists every amendment applied to the STANDARD TERMS.

Typically, parties agree to a derivative contract over the phone. The terms of the oral agreement they reach are documented in the CONFIRMATION. The process is simple: one of the parties documents on paper all of the components of the transaction and forwards it to the counterparty for acceptance. The ISDA provides a standard, plain vanilla CONFIRMATION, which is a short document containing the business terms. If a particular transaction cannot be covered by a plain vanilla confirmation (sometimes called a *structured deal*), the parties must create their own confirmation that is tailored to their needs. In the end, the CONFIRMATION becomes part of the SCHEDULE, which in turn becomes part of the ISDA MASTER AGREEMENT (Figure 8-13).

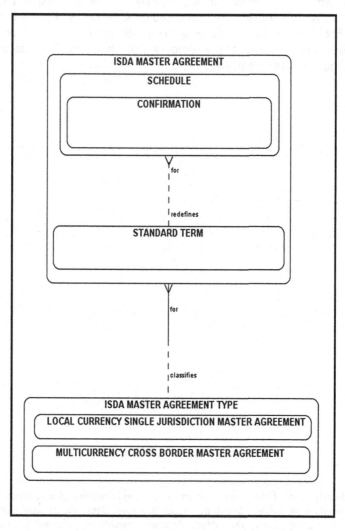

Figure 8-13. Modeling an ISDA document structure (with confirmation)

What happens when data in the SCHEDULE section conflict with the ISDA MASTER AGREEMENT? In this case, the data in the SCHEDULE section win, according to the *inconsistency rule*. The reason for this is simple; the schedule section is where all of the fine-tuning takes place, and thus it overrides the general data that appear in the ISDA MASTER AGREEMENT. What if data in the SCHEDULE section disagree with the CONFIRMATION? Once again, according to the inconsistency rule, the data in the CONFIRMATION section win out.

At this point, you may have already guessed that the internal structure of the ISDA MASTER AGREEMENT document, represented in the model by a document-within-a-document structure, may be modeled using a many-to-many recursive relationship as presented in Chapter 3 (Figure 8-14). The DOCUMENT STRUCTURE allows us to model the complicated document-within-a-document relationship exemplified by the convoluted structure of the ISDA master agreement document.[2]

---

[2]See the descriptions of document metadata and the modeling of document structure in such complicated subject areas as Material Safety Data Sheets and clinical trials observations in David C. Hay, *Data Model Patterns: Conventions of Thought* (Dorset House, 1995; ibid., *Data Model Patterns: A Metadata Map* (Morgan Kaufmann, 2006).

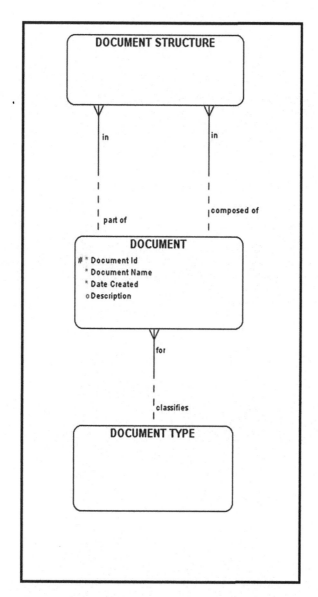

Figure 8-14. Generic representation of an ISDA document structure

Conclusion

This chapter discussed swaps and forward rate agreements, two contract types that are highly popular in the OTC derivatives market and governed by similar sets of business rules. As usual, I modeled these contract types by repurposing modeling patterns developed in previous chapters to these contract-specific business rules.

CHAPTER

9

Parting Thoughts

Nothing is more fairly distributed than common sense: no one thinks he needs more of it than he already has.

—René Descartes, *Le Discours de la Méthode*

I hope that you enjoyed reading this book as much as I enjoyed writing it. In this last chapter I give a few practical pointers that you may find useful in your data modeling career.

What to Do When You Get Stuck

We've all been in situations in which a problem has looked too complex and daunting to tackle. You try to approach the problem from multiple angles but can't come up with any good solutions. In most cases, situations like these arise when you try to solve an entire problem all at once and end up over-complicating it. A better and probably more sensible approach is to break the problem-monolith into smaller parts and tackle them separately. This divide-and-conquer approach has worked wonders for me throughout my career. The effectiveness of this method lies in the fact that by breaking larger problems into smaller chunks, you make them more manageable and easier to solve. Moreover, smaller problems can be more easily fitted into already existing modeling patterns you've successfully used and applied before, resulting in more robust and sensible solutions.

The divide-and-conquer approach is an example of a strategy. Knowledge of sound, workable strategies and ability to be agile in applying them are the trademarks of an excellent modeler. If a strategy does not work, then stop, reassess, and alter it accordingly; otherwise you'll end up wasting your and your users' valuable time.

Implementing Subtype/Supertype in a Physical Data Model

In addition to dividing and conquering, being able to generalize problems is another of the more useful and fundamental strategies in data modeling. When done properly, conceptual-level generalizations improve the overall model quality and facilitate a better articulation of the various business rules.

The time will come, however, when you have to decide how to propagate these subtype/supertype entities from conceptual data models to physical ones. Data modeling practitioners historically have agreed on a number of practical methodologies that deal with subtype/supertype transformations, as discussed in this section.

The main reason we transform supertype/subtype entities in a physical layer is the simple fact that most *relational databases* (RDBs) simply cannot handle them directly. Some databases do provide built-in functionality that indirectly supports subtype/supertype concepts (for instance, Oracle's nested tables). However, this functionality comes with a price; your design may become too difficult to develop, implement, and query.

Because there are multiple ways of transforming subtype/supertypes in a physical data model, you should maintain accurate documentation regarding the reasoning behind performing a particular transformation. At times you may have to backtrack to your conceptual data model, review the reasoning behind a particular transformation, and propose new ways of transforming the supertype/subtype modeling structures.

Figure 9-1 displays the familiar PARTY supertype with two subtypes: PERSON and ORGANIZATION.

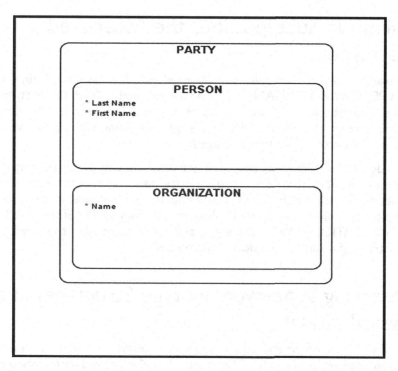

Figure 9-1. Party supertype

The transformation of this supertype structure into a physical layer can be accomplished in several ways, as detailed in the next three sections.

Rolling Down Supertype Structure into the Associated Subtypes

In the approach to transforming this supertype structure into a physical layer that involves rolling down the supertype structure into the associated subtypes, an entity called a PARTY (a supertype) simply ceases to exist. All of the attributes of that PARTY are inherited by its subtypes (in this case, PERSON and ORGANIZATION). In addition to the attributes, each subtype inherits all of the relationships from the associated supertype (an essential detail that novice modelers tend to forget).

■ **Caution**   The finality of the phrase "cease to exist" declares why it is important to maintain the original conceptual model, especially in the event you need to backtrack to the original design.

Rolling Up Subtypes into the Associated Supertype

The transformation that rolls up subtypes into the associated supertype drops PERSON and ORGANIZATION subtypes and rolls up their attributes and relationships into a PARTY table as optional (or nullable). To identify the instances of each discarded subtype, a type column typically is added to separate the person from the organization.

If you decide to follow this approach, you may choose to supplement your solution with database views. These database views can present each subtype independently using SQL SELECT statements. For instance, in the present example you might choose to implement two views: "PERSON_VW" and "ORGANIZATION_VW" (where the suffix VW stands for the *view*), each reconstructing a subtype version of the model.

Preserving Supertype/Subtype Structures in a Physical Model

A third viable transformation is to model all supertype/subtype structures as tables in your physical model. The reasoning behind this decision should be well documented because the resulting structures may lead to confusion or misunderstanding.

Which Option Should You Choose?

Some data modeling practitioners preach the use of one particular transformation methodology and ignore others. I believe this is too restrictive and recommend instead that you keep your eyes and options open. A hybrid approach often provides the most satisfactory results. For instance, you may end up implementing only some of the subtypes and rolling up others. In addition, your particular database platform (and database version) may influence your final decision on how to implement supertype/subtype entities in a physical layer.

Ways to Treat Derived Data

In general, I don't recommended storing and maintaining data that may be easily derived from other, already existing data. First, these data are redundant and take up disk space. Second, the data may be the subject of various data anomalies associated with unnormalized data. The first argument is becoming less important as disk space becomes cheaper. However, various data anomalies can pose serious threats to the integrity of your data and should not be taken lightly. An update—a *data manipulation language* (DML) operation)—to one column may trigger myriad updates to other, dependent columns to keep the data in sync. You will have to make sure that these multiple updates are executed as part of a single database transaction, with a single commit in the end (meaning that either all the updates are successful, or none of them are), if you hope to keep your data consistent. Before you decide on how to store redundant data, do your research and explore all of the available options.

For instance, a good place to calculate derived data is in database views. Database views are lightweight database objects that may be viewed as named database objects pointing to precompiled SQL select statements. The benefit of this approach is that derived data can then be calculated dynamically, on the fly. Its main drawback is the fact that some calculations are extremely resource-intensive and time-consuming. And time-consuming calculations often are reason enough to precalculate and store any derived data in the physical tables. Although this conclusion may seem ambivalent, the topic of derived data is extremely complex, and there are no easy answers regarding its storage in a database.

Don't be afraid to deviate from conventional wisdom and come up with unorthodox solutions. What is appropriate in one case may be damaging in another. My suggestion is to try multiple solutions in the staging area. If a particular approach is too time-consuming and impractical, document it and try other options. Carefully research your database platform, because it may already contain features that you require. For instance, the Oracle database provides materialized views that allow you to preload and refresh (either incrementally or fully) your data, including derived data.

Taking Action

You've probably heard people say that information is power. I don't know about you, but to me information by itself is inert. To make information powerful, you need to act on it. Only with action does information become powerful. We all know from experience that people tend to forget what they don't use. Find a way to apply the knowledge you've acquired by reading this book. Skills that successful data modelers have acquired are a product of hard work and years of dedication. All of us can acquire these skills if we put enough time and passion into studying and practicing them.

Conclusion

Various transformations used in translating conceptual/logical models in a physical layer present their own challenges, and you should carefully weigh your options before committing to a particular design decision. Maintain accurate and up-to-date documentation regarding your conceptual/logical data models, because this documentation will come in handy when you have to backtrack and reexamine your earlier design decisions—especially those made during the translation phase.

I have dedicated the very last section of this book to the importance of taking action. Passively studying something is not enough. Only by practicing and constantly applying knowledge will you gain confidence and recognition in any field.

Recommended Reading

Ralph Kimball and Margy Ross. *The Data Warehouse Toolkit: The Complete Guide to Dimensional Modeling*, 2nd ed. Wiley, 2002.

Richard W. Scamell, and Narayan S. Umanath. *Data Modeling and Database Design*. Cengage Learning, 2007.

Index

A

B

C

Get the eBook for only $10!

Now you can take the weightless companion with you anywhere, anytime. Your purchase of this book entitles you to 3 electronic versions for only $10.

This Apress title will prove so indispensible that you'll want to carry it with you everywhere, which is why we are offering the eBook in 3 formats for only $10 if you have already purchased the print book.

Convenient and fully searchable, the PDF version enables you to easily find and copy code—or perform examples by quickly toggling between instructions and   applications. The MOBI format is ideal for your Kindle, while the ePUB can be utilized on a variety of mobile devices.

Go to www.apress.com/promo/tendollars to purchase your companion eBook.

Other Apress Titles You Will Find Useful

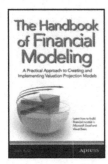

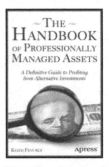

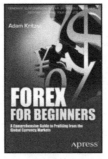

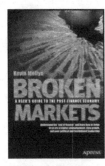
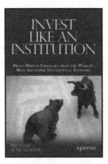
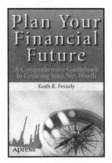